LIVING in the HEART

How to Enter into the Sacred Space within the Heart

by Drunvalo Melchizedek

Living in the Heart

How to Enter into the Sacred Space within the Heart

With two chapters on the
relationship between the heart
and the Mer-Ka-Ba

Drunvalo Melchizedek

Published by
Light Technology Publishing

ISBN 1-891824-43-0

 Published by:
Light Technology Publishing
PO Box 3540
Flagstaff, Arizona 86003
(800) 450-0985

Dedicated to my Love, my wife Claudette

When I met my wife I knew that she held a tradition of understanding the heart that was over four thousand years old. Her teachers Catherine Shainberg and Kolette of Jerusalem trained her in Images of the Heart.

Kolette's lineage goes back to the first people on Earth to write about the Mer-Ka-Ba (Merkavah in Hebrew) in this cycle. But the males of this tribe who were teaching the Mer-Ka-Ba found that their people were not ready for direct interdimensional experience and became extremely emotionally disturbed once they interacted with other worlds directly. In order to solve this problem, the females of this tribe created a system of knowledge to prepare their people for the other worlds by using the female mystery of the Images of the Heart.

When my wife first exposed me to these images, I could find nothing within me to explain what they were or how they were working upon the human soul. All I knew was that they worked.

Over eight years of studying Claudette's work eventually led me in the direction of the research for this book. I feel sure that without her influence I would still be searching for the answers within the mind. And so I am indebted to her, for her Images of the Heart eventually led me to this experience that I am about to share with you. Claudette, I love you and thank you from the bottom of my heart.

—Drunvalo

If someone says to you,
"In the fortified city of the imperishable,
our body, there is a lotus
and in this lotus a tiny space:
what does it contain that one
should desire to know it?"

You must reply:
"As vast as this space without
is the tiny space within your heart:
heaven and earth are found in it,
fire and air, sun and moon,
lightening and the constellations,
whatever belongs to you here below
and all that doesn't,
all this is gathered in that tiny space
within your heart."

* Chandogya Upanishad 8.1.2-3

Given to me by Ron LaPlace the day after this book was finished.

                                     –Drunvalo

Preface

Since 1971, I have been intensely studying meditation and the human lightbody called the Mer-Ka-Ba, and my being has been absorbed in this ancient tradition for most of my adult life. It always seemed to me to be all encompassing and the answer to my myriad questions about life. My inner guidance taught me the sacred geometries that led to my discovery of the lightbody, and sacred geometry itself appeared to be complete and hold all the knowledge and mysteries of the universe. It was truly amazing.

After many years of experience within these fields of light, however, it slowly became clear to me that there was more, yet for a long time I couldn't articulate what it was. As usual, God reveals His/Her Self in unusual and often cryptic ways. Somewhere within the inner worlds of my spaces, an esoteric jewel of immense spiritual value that goes beyond the Mer-Ka-Ba gradually made its way into my life. And for what reason? I can only assume that it was to be used.

So these words are my gift to you, for truly I know who you are and I love you as the Earth loves the Sun. I believe in you, and I believe you will use this knowledge wisely—but I am also not concerned that you might misuse this information, as it cannot be misused.

Drunvalo Melchizedek

Table of Contents

Introruction

L ong, long ago we humans were quite different. We could communicate and experience in ways that only a few in today's modern world would even begin to understand. We could use a form of communication and sensing that does not involve the brain whatsoever but rather comes from a sacred space within the human heart.

In Australia the Aborigines are still connected in an ancient web of life they call dreamtime. In this collective dream or state of consciousness they continue to exist within their hearts and live and breathe in a world that has become almost completely lost to today's Western mind. Nearby, in New Zealand, the Maori can see across the vastness of space to the United States in their "meditations." In this manner they link in actual communication with the Hopi to set up meetings to exchange their prophesies. Without sending a single "technological" communication, the arrangements are made. In Hawaii, the Kahuna commune with Mother Earth to ask for the place where the fish are swimming to feed their people. The billowing white clouds in the pristine blue sky turn into the shape of a human hand that points to the teeming fish below. In a high mountain valley deep in the Sierra Nevada mountains of Colombia, South America, lives a tribe of indigenous people who know the language that has no words. This language comes from a sacred space within their hearts.

If only we could remember! Before Babylon, the Holy Bible says, humankind was blessed with a single language that all peoples on the Earth knew. But afterwards we were split into hundreds of spoken languages creating barriers among us, keeping us separate from one another, each in our own little introverted world.

The mistrust born of misunderstanding was our involuntary fate; in this fashion we were destined to be pitted against each other. We couldn't talk to each other. It was separation in the coldest form. Even if they were born of the same cosmic Source, brothers and sisters were unable to express their thoughts and feelings and soon became enemies. As the centuries piled upon each other, the ancient way of entering the heart to experience the common dream got lost in the isolation of the human mind.

This is a book of remembering. You have always had this place within your heart, and it is still there now. It existed before creation, and it will exist even after the last star shines its brilliant light. At night when you enter your dreams, you leave your mind and enter your sacred space of your heart. But do you remember? Or do you only remember the dream?

Why am I telling you about this "something" that is fading from our memories? What good would it do to find this place again in a world where the greatest religion is science and the logic of the mind? Don't I know that this is a world where emotions and feelings are second-class citizens?

Yes, I do. But my teachers have asked me to remind you who you really are. You are more than just a human being, much more. For within your heart is a place, a sacred place where the world can literally be remade through conscious cocreation. If you really want peace of spirit and if you want to return home, I invite you into the beauty of your own heart. With your permission I will show you what has been shown to me. I will give you the exact instructions to the pathway into your heart, where you and God are intimately one.

It is your choice. But I must warn you: Within this experience resides great responsibility. Life knows when a spirit is born to the higher worlds, and life will use you as all the great masters who have ever lived have been used. If you read this book and do the meditation and then expect nothing to change in your life, you may get caught spiritually napping. Once you have entered the "Light of the Great Darkness," your life will change—eventually, you will remember who you really are; eventually, your life will become a life of service to humanity.

In the last two chapters reside a surprise and a glimpse of great hope. The human lightbody that surrounds the body for about fifty-five to sixty feet in diameter, the Mer-Ka-Ba (which I wrote about in my first two books, *The Ancient Secret of the Flower of Life* volumes I and II), has a secret inherently connected to this sacred space of the heart. If you are practicing the Mer-Ka-Ba meditation in your life, I believe you will find the information in this book to be paramount to your journey of ascension into the higher worlds of light. If you are only interested in the sacred space of the heart, may these words be a blessing in your life and help you remember your true nature.

One last comment. This book is written with the least amount of words possible to convey the meaning and to keep the integrity of the essence of this experience. The images are purposefully simple. It is written from the heart, not the mind.

Chapter One

Beginning with
the Mind

Clearing the Air with Technology

Clearing the Air with the Human Lightbody

Meeting the Inner World in the Heart

Almost at random I chose a seemingly arbitrary point in my life to begin my story: not while I was in meditation of the higher worlds of sacred geometry or the Mer-Ka-Ba, but in a simple everyday scene where I made a decision to help the Earth heal her environment using technology of the mind. I feel we all have this responsibility, and if I was going to talk about it as I did in some of my public lectures, I had to live it. So I opened myself to all the possibilities that might come my way of how I could personally help heal the environmental conditions on our dear Earth.

But so that you understand—it is not the subject of cleaning the environment itself that is the reason why I am telling you this story. It is what happened to me and how my life changed while I was experimenting with an environmental machine called the R-2 that began to open my spirit to a new and different manner of experiencing life.

Little did I know at the time that these technological experiments would lead beyond my mind into uncharted parts of my consciousness and deep into a secret place within my heart.

Clearing the Air with Technology

The story begins in May of 1996, when an old friend called me up and asked if I was interested in helping on an air pollution clearing project he was involved with in Denver, Colorado. I'll keep his name quiet since I believe he would want me to; I'll just call him Jon. This man was a renegade scientist studying all aspects of life and the physical world in a small but sophisticated home lab.

I doubt his IQ could even be measured, as he was clearly a master genius. He had created a new way to "see" into the reality using microwave emissions, which gave him a tremendous advantage in searching for answers in our world. Even our government, knowing his work, was not able to duplicate it until just recently.

Jon said that he and his associates, one of whom was Slim Spurling with his incredible coils, had found out something about nature that could heal some of the environmental problems of the planet, and he wanted me to see what it was. He said that they had cleared up the air pollution in Denver and that the air was now pristine. He asked me to come and see for myself.

I could hardly believe this, since I used to live in Boulder, Colorado, just a few miles from Denver, which had at that time, in the late 70s, the worst air quality in America—worse than Los Angeles even. It was one of the reasons I'd left Boulder in the first place. Actually, I thought Jon might be exaggerating, but knowing his intellect and genius, pretty much anything was possible. So I figured, why not? I needed to get away anyhow, and this looked like something that at the very least would be interesting.

I decided to go with an open mind, with no expectations. Even if what he said wasn't true, this trip would bring me close to the snowcapped mountains of the Rockies, which always made me feel more alive.

❖ ❖ ❖

A week later I stepped off the plane in Denver into a virginal atmosphere the likes of which I had rarely seen in my life. It was more like there was no atmosphere. I could see the trees on the mountains in the far distance, twenty miles away.

I just stood there like a lost tourist in a strange land, gawking at a cleanliness I never saw in the five years I lived there. To say my interest was piqued is putting it mildly; I was stoked. Could Jon really have done this?

An airport taxi crawled up next to me, the driver exuding a soft, relaxed state of mind. He motioned for me to get in the front seat as though I was his old friend, and within minutes we were silently gliding toward Slim Spurling's home and research lab, a place I had never seen before but had heard great stories about.

I remember looking into the taxi driver's eyes, and he seemed to be completely stress-free, an unusual quality for a taxi driver. I asked him how he liked his job. Looking at the road ahead, he said that he loved what he did. To him, people were like open books telling him stories of their experiences as they traveled around the world.

On this note he asked me why I was in Denver. I told him I was there to find an answer to the world's pollution problems. He looked at me, this time with a childlike innocence, and said, "It's all gone now. Look, no air pollution." I told him I could see that the air was amazingly clean. "More than that," he said. "Everyone I know feels so good! Do you know what happened?"

I didn't have an answer to his question, and soon we pulled up to a series of old two-story apartment buildings on the long street that eventually ends at the Colorado School of Mines in Golden, Colorado. Here I was to meet Slim Spurling, one of the researchers compiling the experimental information on a new pollution reduction instrument called the R-2.

This was a magical invention that somehow captured the wave-form of a rain cloud just as it was about to lighten and sent it over a thirty-five mile area, breaking hydrocarbons down into harmless molecules, oxygen and water vapor. Was it really true? It definitely felt like it from breathing the air on Slim's street.

I knocked and heard Slim yell for me to come on in, and so I did. His house was definitely a laboratory and not a place to live, sleep and eat. It soon became clear that his place to live was upstairs, separate from his researching world.

Strange copper coils of various sizes were sitting around the floor, and there were other things that only God and Slim knew what they were. To this man, who looked like a cross between Merlin with his long, white beard and an old cowboy searching for a lost cow to herd home, these "old coils" were actually doing something to help clean up Denver's air pollution.

Jon was not there on the first day but Slim, his co-inventor, and two other researchers who were testing the equipment were. Soon the two left for the day and I was alone with Slim and could begin to understand this man, who was another genius as it rapidly became apparent. I stayed with Slim and his colleagues for a few days learning what they felt they could share with me.

Here is how an R-2 works—actually, there is much more to it, but the following is an approximation: The waveform a rain cloud emits just as it is about to discharge lightning is duplicated in a special machine (this is not the R-2). It is then put on a computer chip in the R-2, whose speaker system sends it into the atmosphere through an embedded coil called a harmonizer. The waveform then grows and expands into the shape of a toroidal field (like a donut), affecting the gravity waves to clean up the pollution from a distance. The R-2 has four dials attached to the end of threaded metal rods, forming a tetrahedron. The dials can be turned to tune the toroidal field so that it "becomes alive."

The heart of the R-2, two of Slim Spurling's coils:
the Harmonizer (left) amd the Acu-Vac (right).

Jon and Slim both considered the toroidal energy fields to be "alive" (and so would I after I witnessed how it interacted with nature). I tried to keep an open mind since much of this was new to me at the time.

First I learned how to tune an R-2 by a feeling in my third eye as I turned the four dials on the unit. Really, it was very easy; as I'd had so much experience in the psychic field, doing this seemed completely natural to me. (Later I realized that only a few could do this right, but almost any sensitive can be trained.)

I continued my training until the day came when Slim and Jon felt that I was ready to test my skills. I was to tune an R-2 in nature and bring a small area of Denver that had gone "out of tuning" back into balance. (If an R-2 goes out of tune, the area it is working on will go back to its original polluted state very quickly, usually within two weeks). At this point, I could hardly believe that any area of Denver could be dirty, but both of them said it was true.

We drove for about twenty miles into the southeastern part of Denver, an area I was not familiar with, and then to the far outer edge of the city; parked the car just off the freeway; and began to walk up the side of a sloping hill to the ridgeline. As we climbed the hill, a small forest emerged toward the top.

I'll never forget what I saw as I reached the top of this hill and looked down into the low, wide valley on the other side. The entire valley was filled with a reddish-brown cloud of pure pollution stretching for several miles. Underneath a small aspen tree, hidden from view to anyone just casually walking by, was an operating R-2 unit quietly singing its melody of a rain cloud. The problem was that it was out of tune.

Jon and Slim told me to sit down in front of the R-2, and they would see if I had learned my lessons. Filled with intense interest and a childlike sense of wonder, I sat down, crossed-legged, in front of the unit and closed my eyes, beginning the meditation and sensing what would tune the unit.

Just as I started to turn the dials, Jon stopped me and said, "Keep your eyes open and watch the pollution cloud." This was not how I had been trained, but I obeyed, watched the cloud and once more started to adjust the dials. Jon stopped me again and said, "Also listen to the birds."

I turned to him and said, "What?" No one had mentioned birds to me during my entire training.

He repeated, "Just listen to the birds. You'll understand."

I had no idea what he was talking about, but I began anyway. As I turned the first dial, I felt the area change for miles around, but nothing happened in the visible world. Once I had adjusted the fourth dial, however, two things happened simultaneously—and both surprised and shocked me.

Instantly, the reddish-brown cloud of pollution disappeared, leaving a clean, clear atmosphere. It was just like a miracle. And at the same moment the cloud disappeared, about a hundred birds began to wildly chirp and sing all around me. I hadn't known they were even there! The two events together had the oddest effect on me psychically. I'd seen and felt the power of the R-2, and in that instant I knew for certain that this new science was real and that I simply had to learn more by direct experience.

During this time, especially in 1995 and early 1996, Denver's air became extremely clean while the R-2 was running, but the city's EPA took full credit for this phenomenon. The agency said that the measures it took were the reasons Denver's air became so clean. However, I watched as the R-2 instantly cleaned large areas of Denver right before my eyes, so I realized that Denver's EPA was simply taking credit for something it had almost nothing to do with.

Further, Jon and Slim had the R-2 tested by an independent lab in Fort Collins, Colorado, which proved beyond a doubt that the R-2 was doing exactly what they claimed it was. The testers had the unit run for a period of time and then they shut it off. They scientifically recorded that the pollution dropped while the R-2 was running and then rose when it was shut off. They did this over and over for a period of, as I remember, about three months. Also, the United States Air Force from Kirkland Air Force Base was watching this experiment as well as the one that I began in Phoenix, which I will speak about soon, and asked if we would submit ourselves and our equipment to their scientific scrutiny. We agreed, and those tests proved conclusively that the R-2 really did clean air pollution.

When we returned to the lab, Jon and Slim sat me down and offered me my very own R-2 to take home to Arizona to experiment with. I have to admit, I felt like a child who had just been given a long awaited toy. I patiently waited to be home, by myself, to begin exploring this unbelievable machine further.

I arrived home to the *Arizona Republic* headlines of May 30, 1996, describing the horrific air pollution problem that had developed in Phoenix. The governor of Arizona, Fife Symington, was saying that the pollution in Phoenix was so bad that the city's classification was about to be upgraded to "serious." Alerts were issued every few days and the situation was growing worse each day.

In response Governor Symington had set up an "Ozone Strategies Task Force," which was headed by attorney Roger Ferland. In reference to finding a solution to the pollution problem, Mr. Ferland said in the Arizona Republic article, "I mean everything. There is nothing we won't consider, no matter how radical or wacky or tough or expensive. We will consider everything."

Mr. Ferland said that they absolutely had to clean up Phoenix; the air pollution was going to destroy the tourist trade and affect almost every business in addition to all the health problems this would cause.

And so I wrote a letter to Mr. Ferland asking for help in setting up the R-2 unit in Phoenix. Since we had scientific evidence that this worked, both from an independent lab and from the United States Air Force, and since we were not asking for financial help, I assumed they would listen to us. Boy, was I wrong! In this letter I simply asked the City of Phoenix to give us a chance to show them that we could do it. We would pay for all costs, and all they had to do was to acknowledge our presence and monitor what we were doing.

I received a phone call from the City by a man named Joe Gibbs, who told me that they were not interested in our R-2 and they would not help in any way whatsoever. You must understand how baffled I was about this response. It was then that I began to realize that the newspaper article was only for show and politics and that they had no intention of actually cleaning up the air pollution in Phoenix. They turned me down on every level.

Fortunately, nobody could stop me from researching, because the R-2 simply runs on a nine-volt battery and uses millivolts to operate, and federal law says that anything that uses less than one volt is unregulated.

So on my own, on June 4, 1996, I turned on the first R-2 in Cave Creek, at the northern edge of Scottsdale. The air was so dirty and dry on that day that it was really hard to breathe. It had not rained for months and months, and even some cacti were dying. For the first three days, nothing happened. Then, on the fourth day, a small, black rain cloud appeared over my house. In all of southern Arizona there was not one cloud, except for this one over my home and the little R-2 unit. Then the cloud began to expand and grow in size.

By the tenth day, the little cloud had grown to about fifteen miles in diameter, and for the first time in a very long while, it began to rain and there was lightning. And man, was there lightning—like I had only seen once or twice before in my life. The storm continued for hours on end, with flashes of lightning moving sideways across the sky. The air had the sensuous smell of ozone. And slowly the sky opened up for a downpour of water. From that moment forth, it continued to rain almost every day, cleaning the sky of pollution and filling the rivers and lakes with fresh water.

By September 1, 1996, the waveform field created by the R-2 was established, and from that day forth there were no more air pollution alerts—not a single one until the U.S. Air Force asked us to shut down the R-2 to see what would happen.

We shut off the machine on May 12, 1998, and already by the end of the month the air pollution had returned and the City had its first alert since 1996. During the time of this test (actually, we'd placed a second R-2 in the City of Phoenix itself in March of 1997, and that is when it began to show results), the hydrocarbon measurements in the City of Phoenix stayed almost always in the single digits. Sometimes, in the middle of downtown Phoenix, the hydro-carbons were measured at zero. There was absolutely nothing, no hydrocarbon pollution. Unfortunately, the R-2 didn't stop the nitrates, which are the cause of ozone pollution, but it really helped with the hydrocarbons. It's all a matter of public record.

By the end of this test, I knew for certain that the R-2 was a success, but the U.S. Air Force, who had been monitoring my actions, entered the picture and asked me to shut down the operation. They wanted to see what would happen and at the same time informed me that the U.S. EPA would never allow what I was doing; they suggested that I go outside of the United States. And so, with the blessings of the U.S. Air Force, I began to experiment in foreign lands.

From June of 1996 to May of 1998 I had performed work with the R-2 and achieved amazing results, none of which the City of Phoenix would recognize.

Finally, I sent another letter to the City of Phoenix:

May 7, 1998
City of Phoenix
Attn: Mayor Skip Rimsza
200 W. Washington
Phoenix, Arizona 85003

Dear Mayor Rimsza:
In May of 1996 an article was written by the Arizona Republic describing how bad the air pollution in Phoenix was and how the future of Phoenix was jeopardized by this problem. In the article, it said that Gov. Fife Symington had set up an Ozone Strategies Task Force which was headed by Attorney Roger Ferland. This article is enclosed. Mr. Ferland said, in referring to the pollution problem, "I mean everything. There is nothing we won't consider, no matter how radical or wacky or tough or expensive. We will consider everything."
At that point I talked with Mr. Joe Gibbs who is on the Ozone Strategies Task Force about the air pollution system that we had been using in Denver, Colorado during 1995. As it turns out, Denver, during the time while we were using our system, had the cleanest year on record ever.
Mr. Gibbs told us that he was not interested in our system, but that because it used less than one watt of energy, there were no laws to stop us from conducting a test if we wanted to. We told Mr. Gibbs that we would do this test entirely at our expense. He still said no. We asked him if he would at least monitor what we were doing, and he refused. I feel he really was not helpful at all. I experienced a very different attitude from Mr. Gibbs than what Mr. Ferland had expressed in the above-mentioned

article. Months later when we tried to give him the independent scientific testing from Fort Collins, Colorado, that proved that our equipment worked, he was too busy. Even when the Air Force, who has also been working with us, called to talk to Mr. Gibbs, he still was not interested.

On June 4th, 1996 we set up a minimal system in Cave Creek which has a range of about 35 miles. It takes three days for the system to turn on, and then about three months for it to become stable. We were fully operational by September 1, 1996. A city like Phoenix should have at least ten units running, but we could not afford to do that. Running one unit is like having a beautiful new car with only 25 horsepower, but it was better than nothing.

Prior to Sept 1, 1996, Phoenix was having an unusually high number of alert days and was about to go into a "Serious" rating by the EPA. But after Sept 1, 1996 I believe we have not had a single alert day. And the pollution has been dropping steadily. In March 1997 another unit was installed near the airport. This gave a much stronger system and affected deeper into Phoenix.

Kirkland Air Force Base in New Mexico has been interested in what we are doing for some time. They have run tests on some of our equipment, and if you are interested in what they think, you can call Lt. Col. Pam Burr at 505—/——.

The reason we are writing this letter is to inform you that we are dismantling our system as of May 12, 1998. We have been letting the system go out of tune for three weeks now. Over the next 90 to 120 days or so, air pollution could return to the way it was prior to June of 1996. Judging by the way the City of Phoenix has responded to this science so far, we do not expect further communication. However, if you find that perhaps we can help you keep our city clean of pollution, please give us a call.

Caring for the Earth,
Dru Melchizedek
General Manager
cc: Lt. Col. Pam Burr
      Arizona Republic
      QED Research, llc
      Gov. Jane Hull

✦ ✦ ✦

During this testing period, I slowly began to understand what was actually happening and how human consciousness was interacting with the R-2 field. I discovered that the R-2 was physically created in the image of the human lightbody, or the Mer-Ka-Ba. Therefore it should be possible for a person who knows the Mer-Ka-Ba meditation and also knows the vibration of the "rain cloud" to combine these two components and then duplicate the action of the R-2 using only pure consciousness without the help of a machine.

I thought about this for hours on end. And one day I found myself in Australia teaching about the Mer-Ka-Ba when one of the students said, "Well, if the R-2 can change the atmosphere over an area, why can't a person who knows the Mer-Ka-Ba do it himself?" My very thoughts . . .

Clearing the Air with the Human Lightbody

There had been a terrible drought in the northern part of the East Coast of Australia. I don't remember the exact timing, but it must have been in '97 or '98. Forest fires were everywhere, with no sign of a letup, and the air hung heavy with the fumes from the raging fires. It was so incredibly dry!

So with this student and about three other people witnessing, I began the meditation of the Mer-Ka-Ba and sent the sound of the waveform of a rain cloud through my Mer-Ka-Ba into the surrounding atmosphere for miles around.

Nothing happened that afternoon, but the following morning we woke up to the sound of rain pounding on the metal roof of our cabin and the sky was filled with mist and high clouds. I jumped up and ran to the window to watch the fierce rain coming down like a waterfall around this little home. The excitement in my heart made me feel like a kid.

I knew it had worked, but at the same time it was only once—and once could simply be a coincidence. The rain continued for three days and hadn't stopped when I had to return to America. Later, when I was back home, I received a call from my friend in Australia who said that after two weeks it was still raining hard. He said that all the forest fires were out and the government declared that the drought was over.

My interest was piqued. Was it really true? Could an ordinary human being change the weather through meditation? A couple of months later, I found myself in Mexico City teaching a group about the Mer-Ka-Ba, when I told the story of the rain in Australia. One of the listeners said, "Well, if you can do it in Australia, will you do it here in

Mexico City? Our air is so polluted that we can hardly breathe."

I have to admit, I have been all over the world, and I have never seen a place where the air was as polluted as it was in this city. I could see no farther than two city blocks before the buildings disappeared. In fact, I could not even see the sky in the middle of the day. It looked like I was living inside a brown dome, and each breath smelled like I was standing behind a diesel truck. This would definitely be a good test.

Accompanied by over forty witnesses, I went to the middle of the city, to an ancient pyramid that was located next to several freeways. We climbed to the top where we could see the city in all directions, but only for a short distance because of the thick pollution.

We sat down in a circle, facing one another on a large, flat, grassy area that was on the top of the pyramid. Everybody knew what I was about to do: begin a meditation using my natural Mer-Ka-Ba field as an antenna to send out the vibration of the waveform of a rain cloud just as it was about to send lightning from its belly. I set my watch, as others did, and began meditating.

The Pyramid in Mexico City.

Fifteen minutes into my meditation, a blue hole opened in the sky, directly above my head. Everyone looked up and pointed. The hole began to grow—and grow it did! After about another fifteen minutes, it had expanded to about two to three miles in diameter. It created a perfectly round hole in the polluted air above the city that looked like someone had used a cookie cutter and chopped out a piece of the pollution from above and just thrown it away.

A "wall" of brown cloud was left in all directions around us, but where we were, in the middle, the air was clean and clear. It smelled like roses, and a beautiful pink cloud formed in the sky above our heads. It was impressive.

For three hours and fifteen minutes, as we recorded it, the wall did not move. The government sent helicopters over the hole to see why it was there, but I never heard what they thought of it. And then, at the end of this time, I told the group that I was going to stop the meditation and to watch what would happen. Immediately after I stopped the meditation, the wall of air pollution began to race toward our group. Within fifteen minutes, it had reached us, enclosing us once again in the terrible stench of Mexico City's exhaust fumes. Once more we were inside a dome of pollution that hid the city from our view.

I remember how I felt in my heart as I was flying back to the United States. I knew beyond any doubt that human consciousness was the answer to all of our problems. I could hardly contain my excitement during the long flight home. After this I performed the same feat again, twice in England and twice in Holland. It worked perfectly each time, and each time in front of an audience of at least fifty people or more. The second time in England changed my life dramatically.

Meeting the Inner World in the Heart

I don't remember exactly where I was in England, but we were at a moor where the Sun had not shone for over six months. The entire landscape was drenched in an everlasting fog that made everything wet and soggy. I was teaching about fifty-five people about the Mer-Ka-Ba, and on the last day of a four-day workshop, I suggested we try the meditation to clear air pollution—but there was no pollution here, only fog. My inner guidance said, "Don't be concerned. Do the meditation and watch what happens."

A moor.

It wasn't easy to convince this English group to go outside into the fog and rain and set up a meditation circle on a wet, grassy field, but they finally agreed. I think they thought I was a little crazy, but somehow they believed me.

They all brought out their umbrellas and sheets of black plastic to sit upon. So here we were, fifty-six people including myself, sitting in a circle in the fog and rain, holding up umbrellas to ward off the elements, looking like fools.

In silence, I began to do the meditation, fully expecting something to happen but not knowing what. After fifteen minutes, a blue hole formed above our heads and began to expand just like it had done in Mexico City. Only this time it expanded much faster and farther, continuing until it was about eight miles in diameter. We were now under a clear, blue sky with the afternoon Sun behind the fog wall that stood like a half-mile-high fence around us in a circle. And then it happened.

A feeling came over everyone in the circle as we all could sense the presence of God. It caused goose bumps on my arms. We looked up into the heavens, and there was the full Moon shining brightly overhead. Only it was different. The sky was so clear that, again, it looked like there was no atmosphere whatsoever. Around the Moon was something else I had never seen but had heard about before: stars . . . stars around the Moon, in the middle of the day! It was awesome.

Suddenly, my attention was directed toward the Earth, and I realized that there were small animals—squirrels, rodents, dogs—all around us, watching. Lots and lots of birds were perched in the nearby trees, singing softly. I looked at the people in the circle, and it was obvious that they were in a state of altered consciousness. I smiled, thinking of St. Francis, and watched the animals all attempting to get as close as they could to us humble human beings.

I remember a thought popping into my head: "I wish we were in the sunshine; it's a little cold." Immediately the entire circle was lit up. I quickly turned toward the source of the light and saw a small miracle in progress. The wall of fog had hidden the Sun, but the moment my desire for warmth surfaced, a hole formed in the fog bank exactly where the Sun was, letting in a ray like a flashlight on a foggy night. And the hole kept pace with the Sun for an hour and a half. Our tiny circle was bathed in the brilliant light as we prayed.

Finally I decided that we had seen enough, and the Sun was going to go down in about twenty minutes anyway. So I told everyone that I was going to stop the meditation. And when I did, the circle of dense fog immediately raced back to where we were. Within minutes, we were enclosed again in the moor's mist and rain.

And as we stood up, a true miracle by anyone's standards took place. A man had come to the workshop with his wife, and he had been in a wheelchair for over ten years. He could stand up, but only for a few seconds, enough time to change position or transfer to another chair, and his wife had helped him all this time. When everyone began leaving the circle, this man stood up from his wheelchair and began to walk back to the lodge with the group, leaving the wheelchair behind! He was walking! It was impossible! He was a little wobbly, but he was walking.

His wife was practically speechless from the experience, but she told me later that not only was he walking, but his spine had also straightened out and he was about six inches taller than he had been before. Joy flooded our hearts and overpowered what had just happened in the field.

As a healer, I have seen miracles many times in my life, but often the malady returns the next day. However, the next morning the man walked into the room for breakfast with his wife beaming at his side. Further, I knew a lady who was their friend, and each year she would call me and give me an update on him. After five years, he was still walking normally.

Here is a case of a man who saw the true nature of reality as a result of the experience in this English field. I believe that he realized that everything is just light and that the world is created from within the human soul; he knew beyond a doubt that he could heal his disease with his own consciousness, and he did.

This experience in England changed my life too, and it took a turn toward an as yet unknown awakening. I began to realize that within the human soul was "something" far greater than anything science or the logical mind had ever considered. The outer world is created by an inner world that I somehow knew was in the human heart—of this I was certain.

I knew this "something" was in the human heart because as I sat in my Mer-Ka-Ba field sending out the vibration of a rain cloud, I could feel the location of the source of the vibration—and it was in my heart; it was achieved by and through the love that I had for Mother Earth. Slowly I was being prepared for a new understanding of my relationship to life.

Chapter Two

Seeing in the Darkness

A Blind Woman Can See

A few years ago, I was friends with Pete Carroll who at that time was the head coach for the New York Jets. He kept telling me that I really needed to meet this woman he knew who was very unusual, who he felt had something to share that I would find important. I was so busy that I put him off for several months. Then one day he asked if he could give her my phone number and have her call me. I agreed, and that is how I met Mary Ann Schinfield, an outstandingly unusual woman. (I mentioned her briefly in the first volume of *The Ancient Secret of the Flower of Life*.)

Mary Ann was completely blind and technically had no eyes, could see absolutely nothing. However, she was able to perform normal everyday tasks—she could even read a book and watch television without any outside assistance.

NASA scientists performed extensive tests to determine how she was able to "see." They asked her what she was seeing inside her head while she was sitting in a room, and she—as she related to me later—told them that she was moving through space and was continuously watching what was going on in the solar system. Even more interesting was that she said she was restricted to this solar system and couldn't leave.

Of course, NASA didn't believe that she was "moving through space," and so they made up a test to see whether she was telling the truth. They asked her to move alongside one of their satellites and give them some kind of a reading from it, a serial number or something. I'm not sure what it was, but she did it precisely, and from that moment on, Mary Ann belonged to NASA. They have never let her go and continue to use her for their own purposes. I don't think I would have played this game with them, but she did.

At any rate, one day she called me, and we began a weekly conversation which we kept up for about four months. I found her to be incredibly interesting in her approach to the nature of the reality we live in, which she perceived as a series of images that originated from within her mind. Never did she think of this reality as "real" in the way most of us do. We talked on the phone every weekend about almost every subject one can think of, always from the point of view of her "images."

One day, after about two months, Mary Ann asked me if I would like to "see" through her eyes. I didn't hesitate and asked her what I should do. She said, "Simply lie down on the bed and make the room as dark as possible."

My wife, Claudette, had been listening in on our conversation, so she lowered the blinds and turned off the lights. It was late at night, at the time of the New Moon, so it was extraordinarily dark anyway. When Claudette was done, I couldn't see my hand in front of my face.

Then Mary Ann told me to get a pillow and prop up the telephone receiver so that my hands were free. I did as she asked. I was now in a completely dark space with my eyes closed, waiting for something to happen. I remember feeling almost jittery with anticipation, for I knew that I was going to experience something new.

After about a minute, she asked me if I saw anything. But there was nothing; it was simply dark like it usually is when I close my eyes. After perhaps another five minutes, she asked again, and there still was nothing. But shortly thereafter, as if a light switch had been turned on, an image appeared all of a sudden in my inner vision. It was that of a television screen, and it was so real that I could hardly believe it.

It was there, and my inner eyes kept scanning this inner TV, for this was something I had never seen before in my whole life. Mary Ann somehow knew I was plugged into her vision, and she remarked, "You can see now, can't you?" All I could respond with was, "Yeah, what is this?" "It's just another way of seeing. Do you see the little screens around the big one?"

In the center I saw a big screen that appeared to be about fourteen inches away from my eyes. Lots of little screens were lined up along its perimeter, perhaps seven little screens along the top and bottom and six along each side. The little screens had very rapidly moving images in them, each one providing information about the central screen.

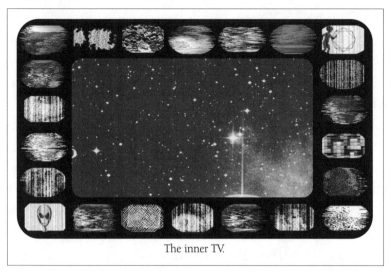

The inner TV.

Mary Ann asked me to look at the top right-hand screen and to look only at that one. I did as she asked. This screen showed images of living beings mixed in with geometric shapes. In other words, I would see, say, a dog followed by a tree and a cube and then the dog with a flower and then an octahedron or some kind of geometric image. It continued in this way, at such speeds that my mind could just barely make out the images.

Mary Ann told me that this little screen showed her what was in the immediate proximity of her physical body—it let her "see" even though she was blind. Amazing!

Mary Ann then invited me to look at the little screen at the bottom left. Again, there were very fast moving images, but they were rather strange. They showed people who didn't look human, and sometimes even dolphins appeared on the screen. Mary Ann said that this was her communication system with her "brothers and sisters" from space and other dimensions. What she meant was ETs!

Before I could think about what I had seen, she asked me to look at the central screen and tell her what I saw. I found myself looking out a window—it was perfectly real, not at all like looking at a TV monitor—and I saw deep space and thousands and thousands of stars everywhere. Never before had I seen the stars like this, and I could "feel" the extreme depth of space in my body. It was exciting, exhilarating.

At that moment, NASA scientists were working with Mary Ann. They had her tracking the twenty-one fragments of comet Shoemaker-Levy 9 that were about to crash into Jupiter. This was back in 1994. The comet fragments were moving behind the Sun at that moment and were about to have a final meeting with their dramatic destiny in astronomical history, by crashing into the surface of Jupiter.

Mary Ann said to me, "Drunvalo, we are about to turn to the right. You will feel it in your body, but don't be concerned." Instantly, I began to feel like I was turning my body, but of course, I was still lying on my bed. The view within the screen began to change, as if I were in a space capsule that was rotating clockwise.

And there, directly in front of me, was one of the comet fragments that the whole world was watching from afar. I don't think we were more than forty feet from this glowing fireball of dust and ice. It was extremely bright and seemed to be standing still. I just stared at this "thing" like I was watching a movie.

Finally, Mary Ann began to speak. "I'm working for NASA at the moment. They want me to answer some of their questions about these comet fragments, but right now I wanted you to see how I see. What do you think?"

Immediately my focus went to another level of this experience. I realized that Mary Ann and I were seeing in the same manner all humans do: We were looking forward, but we couldn't see behind us unless we turned. From past experiences with other life forms I knew that sometimes ETs could see spherically, in all directions at once.

"Mary Ann, what is behind you? Not in the reality you are monitoring, but in the higher reality?" She didn't know. "You know, I have never looked. I've never thought about it." I asked her if it would be all right for me to look and see, and she had no objections. She gave me permission, and so I told her to remain stationary as I looked back.

I turned around to look at what was behind her, and what I saw shocked me so much that even now, after all this time, I feel strange as I relate my experience. Mary Ann had a consciousness that was not human; behind her was the fourth dimension and in front of her was the third dimension. She had a consciousness that was interfacing with both of these dimensions. Until then I hadn't known this was possible.

To describe this experience would be almost impossible unless one has had the experience of the fourth dimension. But all I can say is that the backside of her consciousness was utterly unique. Here was a woman who was unusual in more ways than just being a blind person who could "see." She definitely was not from Earth, that much was clear. I felt sure that if someone were to take a sample of her DNA, anomalies would surface that would point to her origins outside of Earth's biological history.

I continued to talk with Mary Ann for about another two months. After I had experienced the screens, she wanted to talk only in images and symbols, which she asked me to write down. Just like the small screen at the top right of the central screen, her communications were images of living beings mixed with images of geometric shapes. Somehow I always knew what she was saying, even though my conscious mind was having trouble understanding.

Then one day it seemed our relationship was complete and we both said goodbye. I remember thinking that this experience didn't fit into anything I knew, and so I filed it away in what I call my "weird file," waiting for more information to allow newly gained knowledge to connect with other information. But truly, I didn't have any expectations at all. I just added this experience to all the other stuff in my weird file and went on with my life.

China's Psychic Children

I realize that I talked about this in the *Flower of Life* books, but I feel it is important to relate this again for those who did not read them. Back in January 1985, I found an *Omni Magazine* article speaking about superpsychic children in China who had extraordinary abilities. Since the article was in *Omni*, I listened to what they had to say.

Apparently, the Chinese government had requested that *Omni* reporters come and study some of China's psychic children. China was claiming that these children could see with different parts of their bodies while their eyes are sealed off from light; that they could see with their ears, the tips of their noses, their mouths and sometimes with their tongues, hair, armpits, hands and feet.

In 1974 China had found the first young boy who could "see" with his ears. When the boy's eyes were tightly covered, he could still "see" by turning his ears toward what he wanted to see. Then slowly they began to find other children, mostly under fourteen years old, who could see with various parts of their bodies.

This obviously intrigued the editors at *Omni*, and in 1984 they sent a research team to China to study these children. The Chinese government gave the team a group of them to test. The *Omni* article emphasized that the tests were conducted very carefully so as not to be fooled and as if the government was secretly watching their every move.

One of the tests the *Omni* group performed was to take a high stack of books and select one of them at random. Then, again at random, someone would tear out a page and immediately crumple it up into a tight ball before anyone else could see or read it. This crumpled-up page was placed under the armpit of one of the children, also selected at random. Over and over again, the Chinese children could read every word on such pages perfectly! How was this possible? The *Omni* group had no idea. All they could say after testing the children in many ways was that the phenomenon definitely appeared to be real and not sleight of hand.

Inge Bardor—Seeing with Hands and Feet

In the second volume of *The Ancient Secret of the Flower of Life*, I related how Inge Bardor demonstrated her ability to see with her hands and feet during a lecture I held in Denver, Colorado, in 1999.

I had met Inge during a class on the Mer-Ka-Ba meditation I was teaching in Mexico. It was a four-day workshop, and on the third day I found myself talking about the Chinese children who could see with different parts of their bodies.

Suddenly, a young, eighteen-year-old girl stood up and said, "Drunvalo, I can do that. I can see with my hands and feet when I am completely blindfolded. Would you like me to show you?" This was completely unexpected, but of course I wanted her to show me and this group of about a hundred people.

So Inge, all dressed in white and very beautiful, walked up to the area where I was teaching. She immediately asked if there were any skeptics in the group who didn't believe that she could see when her eyes were completely covered. Two young men stood up.

Inge asked them to come on stage with her and told them to fold up two tissues and place them over their eyes in a certain way. Then she wrapped long scarves around their heads to completely seal out any light, and both confirmed that it was 100 percent, totally dark. The two men had removed their scarves and tissues by the time Inge had done the same thing to herself, and she kept the two men there long enough for them to check and make sure she was not cheating. Once they were satisfied that Inge could not see any light, she began.

She sat down on a straight-back chair with her feet flat on the floor and asked if anyone in the room had a photo in a wallet or purse that she could use. One woman took a photo from her purse and gave it to Inge.

Inge immediately turned the photo to face right side up. Her fingertips raced over the surface of the photo for about three seconds, and then she began to describe it to the group as if she had "seen" what it showed. It was a photo of a living room, where four people were sitting on a couch. A large picture was hanging on the wall behind the couch and there was not much else. It was an ordinary, normal photo.

Inge asked, "Would you like me to tell you anything about the people or the house?" This also was something unexpected. The woman who had given Inge the photo asked about the people and Inge stated their names and, if I remember correctly, their ages. The woman was surprised that Inge could know such things and then asked her if she could move through her house.

"I am going down the hallway to the right. The first door on the left is your bedroom." Inge "went" into the bedroom and described the entire room exactly, even telling the woman what was on her nightstand. She then "went" across the hall to the bathroom and again described the room perfectly. The woman was amazed and verified that it was correct.

At that point, one of the two skeptics jumped out of his seat and began to claim that the whole thing was a hoax and that he was going to prove it. He reached into his back pocket to find his wallet, pulled out his driver's license and handed it to Inge upside down and backwards and asked, "Okay, what is this?"

Without hesitation, Inge turned the license around and faced it in the right direction. "This is your driver's license, what do you want to know?" The man said, "Read me the number." And Inge read the number, his address and other basic information off his license. He still was not convinced.

He said to Inge, "Tell me something that only I know and then I will believe you." With a small smile, Inge responded, "You are here with your girlfriend, but you have another girlfriend at home, and her name is . . ." (Inge gave her name to the audience), "and you have been secretly keeping the two apart so they don't know about each other." The young man ripped the driver's license out of Inge's hands and walked back to his girlfriend who was upset after this revelation. He didn't say another word.

Inge continued to demonstrate her abilities until it was downright obvious that her abilities went far beyond simply seeing what was in the photos she was holding in her hands. She could even give the names of the persons who took the photos and what they were wearing or thinking at the moment they pressed the shutter. We all wondered about what we had witnessed. It was real, but how could it be? What was going on?

(Through Inge I discovered that there are two schools near Mexico City that are devoted to teaching children how to "see" with different parts of their bodies as well as other psychic abilities. Inge knew of at least one thousand Mexican children who could see and know in her special way.)

Inge and her mother, Emma, traveled to visit my family and me in Arizona for a few days. We decided to try some psychic tests, and it was fun exploring human potential so directly. What many people thought was make-believe, I was actually witnessing and so were my two children, Mia and Marlee, who were seven and eight years old at the time.

Mia had been quietly watching Inge "see" without her eyes for several hours. Finally she couldn't hold back any longer and she said, "I want to do what you are doing, too, please." Inge turned to her, looked into her eyes and said, "Mia, everyone can do this. Would you like to see like I do?"

Mia jumped up and down, full of excitement: "Yes, yes, yes!" So Inge took her blindfold with the folded tissues and carefully put them on Mia. She kept asking Mia if she could see anything and kept adjusting until Mia said that it was completely dark.

Then Inge thumbed through a stack of magazines for a few minutes until she found just the right photo, a full-page spread of a rhinoceros crossing a blue river that looked like it was taken in Africa. She put the magazine in Mia's lap and placed her hands on the edge of the photo to let her know where it was. Then she simply told Mia to look into the darkness.

After a few minutes, Inge asked Mia what she saw, and Mia said, "I can't see anything. It's all just black." Inge told her to keep looking. After about another five minutes, she moved closer to Mia and placed her fingers on Mia's shoulder. Instantly, Mia exclaimed, "Inge, I can see. It's a photograph of a rionossorus crossing a big, blue river!" Mia couldn't say it right, but we all knew what she was saying.

It was clear that Mia could now "see" like Inge. I asked Inge if she had touched Mia's shoulder at a specific place. She confirmed this and said that she believed she'd become a sort of antenna for Mia so that she could "see." In the school where she learned how to do this, said Inge, they helped her "see" for the first time in the same manner.

Another time, when Inge and I were just talking, I asked her what it looked like inside her head when she was "seeing." For some reason, she hesitated, but I kept prodding her, until finally she explained, "Okay, but it is a little strange, and that's why I didn't want to talk about it. What I see is something like a TV screen, with little screens all around the outside of the screen in the center. The little screens tell me about what is in the center screen."

This was the last thing I'd expected her to say. It hit me like a cast-iron skillet over the head, and the memory of Mary Ann came flooding back into my thoughts. I knew exactly what Inge was talking about, but I'd never applied the idea of Mary Ann's inner screen to the superpsychic children. I couldn't talk for a few minutes.

This meant I had to reanalyze everything I thought I knew about these children. Was it true? Did all superpsychic children see the inner TV screen? According to Inge, at least the one thousand kids in Mexico did.

The Superpsychic Children in China

During the time I was working with Inge Bardor, I was reading about the research of Paul Dong and Thomas E. Rafill, who coauthored the book *China's Super Psychics*. According to them, the Chinese government tested over one hundred thousand children who they had found to be super-psychics who could "see" without using their eyes.

The Chinese government had set up schools to accept these children, when they found them, into special training. Actually, they were both teaching and studying the children in order to understand this great mystery that was unfolding before their eyes.

Mr. Dong reports how these Chinese children were performing incredible feats of psychic abilities while government scientists studied and controlled each experiment to make sure there was no deception.

Here is an example of one such experiment: A bare table was set up in an open area; video cameras were at the ready to record the experiment; and trained scientists were there to monitor any and all movement. One of the scientists placed a sealed and unopened bottle of pills, like vitamins, in the center of the table and a coin or something small like that, perhaps a rock, toward the edge of the table. A small child would approach the table but would not get very close, to make sure he or she could not touch anything. With the child's psychic abilities, the pills would pass through the wall of the glass bottle and end up on the tabletop. Then the other object, the coin or the small rock that was sitting at the edge of the table, would float over to the empty but still sealed bottle and pass right through the glass wall, to be found inside the sealed bottle. This evidently is not too difficult a feat, since over five thousand Chinese children were able to perform this experiment under government scrutiny.

One little six-year-old Chinese girl gave an unusual demonstration of her psychic abilities, with thousands of people in the audience. Before entering the theater, each person was given a rosebud on a stem with leaves. Then the little girl would enter the stage, wave her hands and all the rosebuds in the room would open and become fully mature roses in just a few minutes. If this is a trick, it is a really good one.

There were many different kinds of demonstrations of these children's abilities, but the bottom line was pretty easy to understand: Something extraordinary was taking place in China and in Mexico. Now I had to find out whether this was a planetwide phenomenon or whether it was restricted to these two countries.

Since both Mary Ann and Inge used the same inner screen to see, I had to ask Paul Dong, who had studied these children extensively, about the superpsychic children in China. (Since 1985, there has been extensive research in China around the idea of higher consciousness and psychic phenomena in children that has made its way into such prestigious science magazines as *Nature Journal* and many others. This is something that has been well researched and documented.)

I telephoned Paul in California, where he was living. We talked for about two hours, and toward the end of the conversation I asked him the question that I was so anxious to find out about: "Paul, what do the Chinese superpsychic children see when they have their eyes closed? I mean, what do they see in their minds?"

Paul started acting like Inge had when I'd asked her, saying that it was a little strange and changing the subject. Finally, after at least ten minutes of prodding, Paul ventured to say, "Drunvalo, I have never seen what they see, but the children tell me they see some kind of an inner TV screen on which the images come to them." I immediately asked if there were smaller TV screens around the outer edge of a central screen. Paul said that he didn't know about that; the children had never told him.

So now I knew that the Chinese psychic children also saw some kind of TV screen, but I wasn't sure if it was the same. Yes, this was very exciting. Perhaps what I'd stumbled upon really was a universal phenomenon, and I was now even more determined to find out the truth.

The International Academy of
Human Development near Moscow

One of the Russian reporters and writers of the spiritual webzine *The Spirit of Ma'at*, Kostya Kovalenko, had read one of my articles about the superpsychic children and the inner screen, and he told me that there was a psychic school near Moscow where children are taught to see the inner screen and then to take it even further. The school was making some very powerful claims that, if true, would ultimately change the world forever.

Not only could these children see the inner screen and see without using their eyes, they could even simply hold a book for a few minutes and the entire book would show up on their inner screen. Once there, the children could scroll through the pages like on a computer and read and see all the text and photographs that are in the original book. Further, the children would immediately know the contents of the entire book.

The man who started and runs this school, which is called the International Academy of Human Development, is Viacheslav Bronnikov. The fame and achievements of the school had evidently reached Washington D.C., as Hillary Clinton, during her husband's administration, traveled to Moscow to observe the school firsthand. Did she learn anything? Perhaps that's how she became Senator of New York!

Over the next few months, Kostya told me of two more schools in Russia that were teaching a similar psychic idea but using different teaching methods. It was then that I began to realize that I was on to something that was much bigger than I had originally thought.

In 1999, I went to Moscow myself and was taken to the Kremlin to speak to the Russian Academy of Sciences in Moscow about the human lightbody, the Mer-Ka-Ba. While there I asked about the superpsychic children, and members of the Academy admitted to me that there were thousands of these children in Russia and that many are now about thirty years old. The Russian government has known about the superpsychics for about the same length of time as the Chinese government, since the early 1970s. What an awakening! And I had first thought Mary Ann was just a fluke.

Jimmy Twyman and the Superpsychic Children of Bulgaria

Most of you know James Twyman, who is often called the "Peace Troubadour." He has been traveling around the world singing songs of peace. Several times when Jimmy sang his peace songs, major movements between governments to find peace began. I met James Twyman when he came to my home with Gregg Braden, an old friend, about two years ago. We talked about the superpsychic children, but at that time Jimmy had no knowledge of or experience with these children. And time went by.

Then, in a single day, Jimmy was drawn into the lives of superpsychic children. He was giving a talk to a small group of people in somebody's home. Only adults were initially present, but not long into Jimmy's talk, a young boy of about twelve years of age appeared in the room and sat up front next to Jimmy as he was speaking.

The young boy caught Jimmy's attention, and after a while he found himself giving his lecture directly to the boy. Afterwards the two of them got into a conversation, during which Marcos, the young boy, did something to Jimmy and he saw the inner screen. Jimmy had never seen anything like this before, but he remembered what I had told him and so he called me later that evening to discuss this extraordinary event.

This humble beginning led Jimmy into an amazing adventure, which he describes in his book called *Emissary of Love*. He writes about how he went to Bulgaria, where Marcos was from, and eventually found a monastery high up in the mountains where the monks were training children to see the inner screen and to see with different parts of their bodies.

These children from Bulgaria are now speaking with Jimmy telepathically about how the world can come to peace. Their primary message is that peace lives within each of us and that we are in truth emissaries of love. And from this understanding they want to ask us one question: "If we see ourselves as emissaries of love, then how do we live our lives, knowing this truth?" And they tell us, "Begin now."

It was slowly becoming clear to me that somehow seeing in darkness was a fact, though I still didn't really understand it. I was learning that we can see with light using our eyes and our mind, or we can see with another part of ourselves using darkness; I was learning that we can even see and know far more than just the surface of things. Where this was leading, I really didn't know, but I'd always trusted in Great Spirit and knew that everything is whole, complete and perfect just as it is. I knew that I just had to wait and keep my awareness open and the truth would reveal itself.

Chapter Three

Learning from Indigenous Tribes

Aboriginal Elders Share Their Energy

The Power of a Maori Prayer Coming from the Heart

The Kogi Experience

The Colombian Woman

Becoming One with Horses

Taking Another Person into the Sacred Space

hile all these experiences around the superpsychic children were occurring in my life, another related strand threaded its way into my study of seeing in darkness. It was very subtle but ultimately paramount to the experience of where all this was leading—the secret, hidden place within the heart that generated these incredible images the children were seeing and gave them their knowledge.

Slowly, indigenous tribes from all over the world came forth with yet another piece of the great mystery, nudging me to remember something ancient about my spirit. Members of many tribes told me they were hoping that through me, change would begin within the technological world that would lead to world peace and environmental balance.

Aboriginal Elders Share Their Energy

In the mid 1990s, I was asked to talk at the Dolphin & Whale Conference in Australia. I arrived in Queensland to be immersed in the beauty of this land with its Great Barrier Reef, which is over one thousand miles long. What a fantastic place to be alive in!

Hundreds of people from all over the world were there to discuss dolphins and whales, but also to talk about related subjects, like the world's environment. (Obviously, the dolphins and whales and the rest of life are not going to survive unless we humans change our course in how we are living.)

I was at that time experimenting with the R-2s and had finally discovered that a single person, connected to Mother Earth, could change the environment by using his or her lightbody, or the Mer-Ka-Ba. I was very excited about this concept, and when it was my turn on stage, knowing who my audience was, I spoke about it from a very personal point of view. I emphasized that our thoughts and emotions can create the world around us and that by staying connected to Mother Earth within the heart, all things were possible— even cleaning the environment with only the human lightbody.

At the end of my talk, I stepped off the stage, walked to the back of the room and waited to hear the next speaker. But I was intercepted by a group of five or six elderly Aboriginal men. They motioned for me to come over to their circle, which I did without thinking much about it.

These old men took me in their midst and told me that I was the first white man they had ever heard speak the truth as they knew it. They told me how Mother Earth provided everything to them without their having to struggle, that the world was just light and that human consciousness was more than whites usually understand. (They consider us a mutation of their consciousness, just babies who are still learning about the outer world.) The old men told me that they were going to support me while I was in Australia if I agreed to allow their help. I didn't really understand what they meant by "support," but of course I agreed—after all, they truly are our elders.

After that I decided to speak in other Australian cities, such as Brisbane, Melbourne and Sydney. And each time when I began my talk, I would look out into the audience and there would be these old men sitting in the back of the room in a circle, chanting softly. Some of my audiences consisted of well over a thousand people, but the energies coming from these old men were so strong I could feel them almost pulsating in the room. I don't know how they found me or even how they were able to travel these great distances since they didn't own cars, but they were always there.

They told me one last thing before I left their circle at the Dolphin & Whale Conference: "Remember the darkness and the heart when you create." At that time, it meant nothing to me.

The Power of a Maori Prayer Coming from the Heart

Soon after I returned home from Australia, the spiritual leader of the Waitaha Maori, the indigenous people of New Zealand, asked me for permission to come to my home in America and talk with me. Macki Ruka made this request through Mary Thunder, a Native

American elder who called me and drove him to my home. This was pretty interesting, since I'd had no contact with these people, but there was no way I was going to turn him down, even though I had no idea why he wanted to talk with me. Mary Thunder brought Macki Ruka to my home along with several of his assistants. Mary is a wonderful grandmother of the Cheyenne tribe, and we have remained friends ever since.

Macki Ruka was an impressive man weighing about three hundred and fifty pounds. He brought several young men from his tribe with him to carry all the sacred ceremonial items he felt were necessary for his visit with me. Some of these items weighed over a hundred pounds! I can't remember exactly what they were except they were very heavy as it sometimes took more than one person to move them. The ceremonial articles were placed all around us as we began to speak.

Our conversation soon led into a discussion about the survival of the world and how we, members of modern civilization, needed to remember the old wisdom to survive. He said clearly that there were forms of communication that, if remembered, would change everything in the world. For some reason, it was clear that this was his primary message. We talked for about four hours about many subjects, but before he left, he told me that he was going to send someone from his tribe to me and for me to wait for this person. I didn't understand why he was doing this, either, but I agreed.

A few years later I was living with my family in Arizona and we were in the middle of a move from Sedona to Cave Creek. I had rented a moving van and was struggling to lift box after box into the van. (You would not believe how much stuff I had acquired once I was married. When we met, Claudette had a house full of everything necessary for life and so did I.)

As I was slowly trudging back and forth between our home and the van, moving more and more stuff out of the house and loading it up, a young man I had never seen before walked up to me. "Hi," he greeted me. "Do you need help loading your truck?" He was about twenty-eight years old and spoke with a perfect Californian accent. He wore old blue jeans and a clean white tee shirt and a big smile. As a matter of fact, he could have been one of my neighbors back when I lived in California as a child and young adult.

I told him, "No, that's okay. I don't have too much left." Actually, I really did need his help, but I didn't want to impose upon his friendliness. He looked me straight in the eyes and from his heart gently insisted, "Really, I have nothing to do and I would enjoy helping you." How could I refuse?

So we began to work. He didn't have much to say but seemed to simply focus on the work and do it. And so, in near silence, we worked together. When the truck was fully packed, I thanked him and asked if there was anything I could do for him. He said, "No, but I really would like to help you unload your truck at your new home. Is that okay?"

I couldn't believe such generosity. "No, that's too much to ask. But thank you for everything you've done." And again he looked into my eyes and said, "Please, let me help you. You need my help, and I have absolutely nothing else to do. Really, it's okay." Somehow I began to feel like I knew him from somewhere. He felt like a brother in my heart, and so I surrendered to his plea. "Okay, jump in. But you're crazy."

It was a two-and-a-half hour drive to our new home, so there was ample opportunity to ask him many questions about himself. When he'd helped me load, he'd said almost nothing about himself, but now he was held captive in this old, rented truck.

We were barely outside Sedona when I asked were he was from. I expected him to answer "California," but instead he said, "From New Zealand." No further explanation. I looked at him, surprised. "I thought you were from California. Did you live there for a while?" Without looking at me, he replied, "No, this is the first time I've ever been to America. I arrived about two weeks ago."

Immediately I turned to him and inquired, "Well, where did you learn to speak English with a Californian accent so perfectly?" His reply shook me to my bones. "Oh, I just learned it about three weeks ago. My tribe taught me." My curiosity jumped into awareness. "What!? You learned perfect English in less than a month?" "Yes, it was easy."

Then, before I could rebound from his incredible statement, he said, "Do you remember Macki Ruka? He sent me to you." I had almost completely forgotten Macki Ruka's promise to send someone to me, so this caught me completely off guard; I couldn't even say, "You're kidding me." And that would have been ridiculous anyway. No one could come up with those words about having been sent by Macki Ruka unless they were true. No one knew, except me.

Instantly I realized that I was in the midst of a deeply spiritual experience; the energy in my body changed. I turned to him and asked, "How did you find me?" His reply was so obvious, "Easy, I followed my heart."

After a pause he continued, "Actually, I first had to go to the Hopi. I was instructed that my tribe and the Hopi were to share prophecies and I was elected to go to them. Afterwards I was told to find you. I went straight to the Hopi. Can I tell you what happened there?" As if I was going to stop him! He told me a story that few would believe, but I tell you, this is exactly what he said:

He adjusted himself in the seat of the old truck and turned slightly toward me. "I arrived at Third Mesa late at night. But they [the Hopi] somehow knew I was coming, and a place for me to stay was prepared. The next day they took me into one of their kivas and kept me there for three days and nights. We were in complete darkness.

"To convey simple requests, they spoke Spanish, which I also know, but mostly they spoke to me in visions and images, revealing their prophesies. I related back to them our truths about what the future will hold. Then, on the third night, they handed me an old clay pot and asked me what I felt about it.

"Really, at first it meant nothing to me, but after holding it for a few hours, a wave of knowing came over me and a tremendous vision followed. I could see that I used to be Hopi hundreds of years ago and that I was the person who had made this pot. I also remembered that I had placed an image into the pot for myself to remember hundreds of years into the future.

"In this vision I remembered everything about myself and my life living with the Hopi. It was so satisfying and so amazing to remember everything. I also instantly remembered how to speak the Hopi language. From that moment on we only spoke Hopi. That was three days ago."

What can you say to something like that? After a pause I asked, "Could you tell me what was shared in the prophecies?" He looked at me like he really wanted to, but he answered, "I'm sorry, but I'm not allowed to talk about the prophecies with anyone."

And so the conversation drifted to his ordinary experiences in the States since his arrival. He thought this was an unusual place to live. He felt we were too far removed from nature and reality, and TV he considered to be "mind masturbation."

Soon we arrived at our destination and pulled the truck to a stop in our new driveway. Again, he spoke little and worked hard as we unloaded our things. When we were finished, he asked permission to perform a ceremony on the new land before we returned to Sedona. In time this ceremony turned out to be a grand lesson in the power of prayer, especially when this prayer comes from the heart.

The land we had purchased was of a near-perfect pentagon shape. My Maori friend asked if he could pray at each of the five points, and of course I gave him my permission. Together we went to each of the points and he prayed with deep reverence: "Beloved Creator, please hear my prayer for my friend Drunvalo." He continued asking that all the animals would find refuge on this land; that everyone who lived here would be healthy, happy and never get hurt; and finally that no one would ever take this land from me. There was more in his words, but this was the essence.

Soon afterward we returned to Sedona where he gave me a big hug, looked into my eyes for one last time and left. I never saw him again.

When we moved into our new home, my wife and I noticed that animals were sleeping all over our land. We only had one acre and about half of that was walled in for the house. But as little room as there was, animals who normally would not be near one another, such as deer, javelinas and coyotes, slept in close proximity. In fact, coyotes usually sleep inside the Earth, but not here—they would sleep only a few feet from each other. We often laughed about the Maori prayer that brought so many different kinds of animals to us. And even though there were vast numbers of scorpions, rattlesnakes and Gila monsters all over our land, no one was ever bitten or hurt.

After about three and a half years, we decided to move to another home. Our house was located in an extremely popular area and the realtor had utmost confidence that our house would sell in two weeks and definitely within thirty days. But after almost a year and hundreds of prospective buyers we still had not sold our beautiful house. We didn't know what to do.

One night Claudette woke up out of a dream and said, "Drunvalo, remember what the Maori said, that no one would take our property? We must break this prayer or our home will never be sold." The next day, together, we went to each of the five points on the land and prayed to change the Maori's words. Our house sold five days later.

The Kogi Experience

It was with the Kogi that my experiences with indigenous peoples began to manifest more than just lessons in spirituality and human potential. What they taught and showed me illuminated the spiritual idea of being able to see within darkness. Without their help, I might never have found this secret space within the heart. For their loving assistance, I will forever be indebted to them.

I had just finished an Earth/Sky workshop in Maryland, U.S., when a young white man approached me and said that he was sent by the Maya of Guatemala to give me a message from the Kogi tribe of the Sierra Nevada Mountains of Colombia, South America. I listened to him, but I had never heard of the Kogi tribe.

A Kogi village.

He explained that the Kogi were one of the few tribes who mostly escaped the Spanish Inquisition in the 1500s, by moving high up into the Sierra Nevada de Santa Marta. There they were inaccessible and therefore able to maintain some of their original culture and religious beliefs. Even now, they live almost the same way they did a thousand years ago.

Within their tribe is a group called the Mamas, who the Kogi believe are not really human but part of the Earth's consciousness that maintains the balance of the world's ecological system. The Kogi believe that without the Mamas, the Earth would die.

The Mamas are also the religious leaders of the Kogi tribe and are respected in the same way Jesus is respected by the Christians or Mohammed by Muslims. According to the young man who was telling me this story, the Mamas are able to see in complete darkness, and they watch over the world with their inner vision and their intimate connection to Mother Earth, who they call Aluna.

Kogis.

What is incredibly interesting is that when a baby who is or will become a Mama is discovered within the Kogi tribe, it is taken to an unusual place for special training and upbringing. In the old days, this was a completely dark cave, but today the baby is taken to a special building constructed of all natural materials where no light can enter. In almost complete darkness, this special baby will be fed only white foods while it grows up and will be given just enough light so as not to go blind. The baby also receives a most unusual spiritual training. For nine years this baby remains in complete darkness, learning to see without using the eyes, just like the superpsychic children who are emerging around the world. At nine years of age, the young child is brought out into the light to learn how to see with the eyes. What an experience that must be! Can you imagine what it must be like to see this incredible planet for the first time when you're nine years old?

The young man who was telling me about the Kogi and the Mamas began to tell me another story, about why he was sent to me. He said that the Kogi Mamas were not only able to see anyplace in the world, but they could also see into the future, just like the Hopi, the Maori and many other indigenous tribes around the world. He said that the Kogi Mamas had never been wrong in their predictions about the future in their entire history.

According to the Kogi Mamas, by the last solar eclipse of the twentieth century, on August 11, 1999, all the techno-cultural peoples of the world should have gone to another dimension of the Earth's consciousness, leaving behind the indigenous and natural peoples of the world to inherit the physical planet. (This is reminiscent of the Bible's words that the "meek shall inherit the earth." This prediction is also very similar to what Edgar Cayce, the "sleeping prophet," said, that by the winter of 1998 the poles of the Earth would shift and an enormous change would happen on Earth. Many New Age people thought this meant that most of the consciousness of the world would move into the fourth dimension.)

The young man moved closer to me as if to emphasize what he was about to tell me. He lowered his voice and whispered, "On August 12, 1999, the Kogi Mamas saw that we, the techno-culture, were still here on Earth. They went into deep meditation to see why, since this was the first time in their long history that one of their predictions didn't come true."

According to him, there in the darkness the Kogi Mamas could see lights all over the surface of the planet—and they had not been there before. In investigating these lights, the Mamas found that they were the lights of people who had learned about their lightbodies, which in ancient times were called "Mer-Ka-Bas." It was the Mamas' belief that these people with their lightbodies had changed the course of history.

As a teacher of the science of the Mer-Ka-Ba, I know that once we remember our Mer-Ka-Ba, we can, with certain training, alter the external world by what we think and feel. According to the Kogi Mamas, some of us did change the outer world so much that a new reality was created. And this was something the Kogi Mamas had not seen, because it originated in the future, not in the past. Of course, if this is true, it begins to reveal an even deeper level of the nature of human potential. (Just so you know, the Kogi Mamas hadn't thought we knew how to use this ability within us.)

Here is an interesting piece of information. The United States Air Force had contacted me when I was working on clearing up air pollution, first with the R-2 and then using my Mer-Ka-Ba, and in personal discussions, they revealed something very interesting. Many of my Mer-Ka-Ba students have been telling me—and I myself have seen this—that the moment they activated their Mer-Ka-Ba for the first time, they sometimes found themselves surrounded by black helicopters. And often the helicopters simply would not go away but follow them around and stay with them for weeks or even months. A major in the Air Force told me that as the Mer-Ka-Ba disk expands, one person in his or her Mer-Ka-Ba field puts out about the same energy (magnetic pulse) as a city of about fifteen thousand people. She said that their satellites could see a person's lightbody and show the image on the Air Force's computer screens. For several years this caused a huge concern in the U.S. military, but now they understand that this is simply part of the new consciousness that is unfolding on Earth at this time. So if the U.S. Air Force can "see" the Mer-Ka-Ba field, why not the Kogi Mamas?

The young man looked at me innocently and said, "The Kogi Mamas wish to thank you for teaching about the Mer-Ka-Ba and changing the world in the process." He then handed me a small package of tobacco wrapped in a bright red cotton cloth as a gift from the Mamas to show their appreciation. I was not prepared for this unexpected ceremony, so I glanced around and gave him a red rose from a nearby flower arrangement to give back to the Mamas. And then it was over.

After he'd left, I thought about this experience for a while, but I soon forgot about the Kogi as my thoughts returned to the familiar world of my life. I never thought that I would ever hear from them again.

A couple of months went by and after yet another workshop, this same man approached me, again with a message from the Kogi Mamas. He said that the Kogi Mamas wanted to meet with me and teach me the "language that has no words." He then told me that it would be very unusual for them to come to the United States, as only three of them had ever left Colombia, but if I asked, they would find a way. They really would like for me to come down to the Sierra Nevada de Santa Marta and meet with them there.

I thought about this message for a while and then went into a deep meditation asking my two angels permission to embark on this new adventure. Both looked at me and immediately gave me permission to pursue this experience, whatever it was going to be. I opened my eyes and simply said, "Yes, I will allow this."

I had the option of either going to the mountains of Colombia or having the Mamas find me. Knowing my supertight schedule was booked solid for the next year, I asked if they could come to me. Without hesitation the man responded, "I will relay the message," and left without another word.

On my way home on the plane, I finally had time to think about this. Although I didn't know how the Kogi Mamas were going to find me, I was sure they would. I have personally seen indigenous people interact in this ordinary world in ways that most people would find hard to believe. Here is one example:

The people of Taos Pueblo in New Mexico had asked me to participate in a ceremony to help heal the pain between white and red man. The ceremony was to be performed by the followers of the peyote cult, the Native American Church, within the Taos Pueblo and was set to commence on the sunrise on a certain day in the future.

The day arrived and the Sun was just about to break over the edge of the horizon, when three Huichol Indian shamans arrived at our ceremonial circle and asked permission to participate. They were dressed in full ceremonial dress, with feathers in their hair and paint on their faces and bodies.

Jimmy Reyna, a native of Taos Pueblo who was leading the ceremony, asked them how they had known about this ceremony, because those involved in it had been asked not to tell anyone. They said they'd been in a peyote ceremony in Mexico and saw the vision of this ceremony. Their leaders determined that these three men were to go to our ceremony, so they dressed for the occasion and walked all the way to Taos Pueblo.

Pretty impressive, since they lived three hundred miles from the U.S. border, and once they crossed, they still had to walk another three hundred miles to reach Taos Pueblo—six hundred miles and no one stopped them! They crossed the Rio Grande; they walked over freeways; they climbed over barbwire fences; and they arrived only about five minutes before we began the ceremony—all this in full ceremonial garb. Life and human potential are so much greater than most people accept.

And so I waited for the Kogi Mamas to contact me somehow, although I couldn't image how it would happen.

The Colombian Woman

Two or three months later, I found myself in Cuernavaca, Mexico, not far from Mexico City, giving another Earth/Sky workshop. A little over one hundred people were present and about twenty of them happened to be from Colombia.

One of these Colombians, a woman in her early forties, seemed like any other modern woman, until our group would perform a ceremony, a dance or a chant that was "real," meaning something that made the people aware of the presence of God. At that point, her personality would change completely. She became uninhibited and primitive; she would dance with the movements, abandon and intensity of one who had given herself over to the chanting and music—not something you would expect from a modern woman.

To me it was beautiful to watch her, but the other Colombians were embarrassed by her actions. As this woman continued with her "unusual mannerisms" every single day of the four-day workshop, the others in her group became more and more impatient with her.

On the third day, the group was in a large circle holding hands and chanting certain sounds to heighten awareness. In her unusual nature, this woman broke the circle and went into the center, wildly dancing to the chanting. After about fifteen minutes, the Colombians couldn't stand it anymore and motioned for me to stop her. I didn't really want to because her movements were so beautiful to me. However, out of respect for the others, I entered the center of the circle to take her back to the group.

As I approached her, she was facing away from me. I lightly touched her on the shoulder, and she spun around. She looked past my eyes into my soul, and her body emitted this strange sound that seemed to surround my body. Instantly I was no longer in a room in Cuernavaca. I was in a foreign place with grass huts and people standing around in white clothing, looking at me. It was as real as reality. A dog even ran by.

I was not in my own body anymore, but in a female body watching the surroundings. A strange, unknown feeling surged through me that felt almost sexual, yet wasn't. Let's just say it felt really, really good. And then, just as I was beginning to accept my new reality, I suddenly found myself back in the room in Cuernavaca looking into the eyes of this very strange woman. I had never had an experience like that before—and I've had some pretty unusual experiences.

At that moment all I knew was that I wanted to feel that way again. So entirely giving up my place as leader of the group and in the middle of the chanting, I took the woman by the hand and headed for a corner in the huge room. I sat her down, looked into her open, brown eyes and said, "Please do that again."

The woman smiled and made the sound again, and once more I was no longer in Cuernavaca, Mexico—I was in Colombia. For two hours, according to the people in the group, who had stopped chanting and were watching, I was in an altered state of consciousness.

In the short time I spent with her, I learned and understood what was really going on. It became so clear to me. Actually, two old Kogi Mamas explained it to me while I was in this female body in Colombia.

They said, "We traveled down the mountain to another tribe nearby, to a woman in that tribe who has special abilities. We asked if she would help us reach you, and she agreed."

Apparently, the woman, whose name was Ema, laid down on a bed made of thick grass, in a round grass hut. Her spirit left her body and traveled farther down the mountain, to the bottom where a Colombian woman was living in an old Spanish adobe house. Ema entered this woman's body—I don't know if she had permission to do so—and put the idea into her mind to go to my workshop in Mexico so that she, Ema, could teach me the "language that has no words."

What is even more interesting is that the Colombian woman had no money, no passport or visa, no birth certificate or any other manner to prove her identity and no airline ticket. Yet she managed to find her way to Mexico to come to the workshop. Someone bought her an airline ticket, and before I left the U.S., the angels had told me to give her a free workshop. But still, how did she get through customs without any identification? How did she manage to travel from Colombia to Mexico and back again by air with no complications? I guess they just couldn't "see" her.

What I was learning from Ema with her strange sounds in the corner of the room was far more than just how the Kogi Mamas did this spatial transformation with me. With my newly found abilities, I was walking around in the real world on Kogi land, in a female body, with old Mama shamans all around me. I knew that they knew it was me in this body, and one by one these shamans would come very close to my face and make strange sounds.

Each time a sound was made I would immediately disappear into yet another reality where they began to teach me about their history, culture and spiritual beliefs. By the time this very real experience was over, I knew everything about this woman whose body I was using. I knew her husband and three children as though they were mine. Two old Mamas were by my side throughout the whole experience, and I came to know them like they were family.

One of them was Mamos Bernardo, and he became my guide over the next few months. I felt like I had just been reborn into a new, incredible world where all the old rules had been thrown out. My old, familiar world seemed more like a dream than reality, whereas this new world was real.

My session with Ema ended as suddenly as it had begun, and I was back in my own body in Mexico, giving a workshop about something that at that time I thought was totally unrelated.

Slowly, over the next few weeks, I began to understand my new experience and began to accept the way the Kogi Mamas were teaching me so gracefully. I learned that the sounds came not from the mind, by thinking and words, but from the heart, from a sacred space within the heart; they were directed by dreaming and feelings and emotions. (Both mind and heart produce images in the body, but only the heart creates images that seem completely real.)

Here was definitely a means of communication that went far beyond anything the mind was capable of. I had just experienced the "language that has no words," and I was never going to be the same again. I felt simultaneously honored and excited about the possibilities. The language with no words could also be used as communication between all life forms—not just between humans. The Kogi Mamas told me to try communicating in this manner with animals so I could see this truth for myself.

Becoming One with Horses

Claudette had three horses that lived in a huge, open field. The day after I had returned from Mexico, I grabbed her hand and pulled her outside to go and see them. I had already told her about my experiences with Ema, and we both wanted to see what would happen.

We arrived at the field to find the horses lazily standing by the fences about a hundred feet apart, ignoring one another. I slowly walked out into the middle of the field as Claudette prepared to feed them. All three of them seemed to be asleep under the hot, dry Arizona sunshine.

Quietly I moved out of my mind and into my heart as I had been taught, and this high-pitched sound came out of my body. I didn't make the sound—it just came out and the image of a baby colt appeared in my inner vision.

Instantly all three horses jerked their heads around and pinned their eyes on me. Then, as if on cue, they all began to run as fast as they could toward me. When they reached me, one after another pushed its face up against mine. In a matter of seconds I was surrounded by a world of horses, trapped in the middle. As if on a hidden sign, they all lowered their heads together and I had no choice but to follow their lead.

For the next thirty minutes I became a horse. We made little sounds to one another, interspersed with quiet whinnies. Images of horses and herds filled my being and the same "sexual" feeling I had experienced with Ema flooded my body. I can't fully explain it, but it was one of the most rewarding moments in my life, and I was overwhelmed with joy to be talking with these horses.

And then, as quickly as it had begun, it was over. But I had changed forever and so had the horses. From then on, my relationship with them was no longer one of man and horse—it was one of family member to family member. What a gift! And in that moment I knew with absolute certainty that my experience in Mexico had been real. Life was getting really good!

For those of you who know the Christian Bible, remember the story of Babylon? According to the Bible, before Babylon the whole world spoke one language and humans could even speak with the animals using this language. After Babylon, God separated us into many languages, which has been keeping us apart because we can't always understand each other. However, archaeologists have never discovered any trace of this one language anywhere in the world. Why?

I believe it is because this one language is not a language that is written or spoken with words, but rather it is created by sounds from within the heart. Only when the heart of humankind opens again will we remember the language and be reconnected—not only among ourselves and with the animals, but to all life everywhere.

Taking Another Person into the Sacred Space

About two weeks after my experience with Claudette's horses, I was at the East Coast to give another Earth/Sky workshop. What I had been learning from the Kogi Mamas was still foremost in my mind. My facilitator, who was helping me set up the workshop, listened closely to what I was saying about this sacred space within the heart, and finally she could not contain herself anymore. She asked, "Could you please show me?"

At first I was reluctant, because we humans have much emotional garbage and control restraints, which makes leaving the mind scary for most of us. But she was persistent and finally I consented to try, not really expecting anything to happen.

We sat cross-legged, facing each other, and began with a simple meditation of watching our breaths, more to relax than for anything else. Then, as the Kogi Mamas had shown me, my spirit literally left the space of my mind and moved into my heart, and almost immediately strange sounds came out of my body and an inner vision appeared.

I found myself just a few feet from the muddy-green Amazon River with a massive jungle tree off to my left. The tree had an enormous branch that ran parallel to the ground and extended about twenty feet from the main trunk. With my spirit about six feet off the ground I observed directly below me a large male puma walking swiftly and with determination. The animal leaped up onto the enormous branch and cat-walked almost to the end. From there it jumped agilely to the ground and continued walking along the river.

The next moment I was back in the room with my facilitator. I opened my eyes and she opened hers at the same time. I looked at her to see what she had experienced, but didn't expect anything. To my total surprise, she described my experience, down to the smallest detail. I could hardly believe it. It worked! Leaving me no time to think about what had just happened, she excitedly asked me to do it again. She reminded me of how I had felt when Ema had first made the sounds for me.

So we closed our eyes again and in a moment another sound came out of my body. Immediately I was at the ceiling of a room in the Colombian woman's house, looking down at her as she was sleeping in her bed. It was early in the morning and her home was old and made of adobe.

The spirit of Ema rolled out of the Colombian woman's body and rose to join me at the ceiling. We merged and together went right through the wall to the outside. We rose high into the air where we could see the jungle below us and the mountains all around us.

Then, like a jet plane, we began to rapidly move over the treetops and headed up the mountain. We flew at a tremendous speed, staying maybe one hundred feet above the trees clinging to the sides of the rising mountains until finally we dropped over a ridgeline down into a high mountain valley, where a village of round straw huts nestled.

We flew straight to one of the huts and passed right through the walls to where Ema's body was lying naked on a bed of grass. (Usually the Kogi and the other tribes on this mountain sleep in hand-woven hammocks, but they were concerned about leaving Ema in a hammock over an extended period of time without her consciousness.)

We rolled into her body, and she woke up to her family standing all around her. Her three children came running, excitedly yelling her name to give her a hug for returning. The youngest, who was just over a year old, went immediately for her left breast and begun suckling. Her husband and two old Mamas stood by. I looked at them, and they acknowledged my presence. And then it was over.

I was back in the room at the East Coast of the U.S. with my facilitator. Again we both opened our eyes at the same moment. Without me saying a word, she began to describe the experience in perfect detail, with one exception, which to this day I don't understand. She saw Ema's spirit coming out of the Colombian woman's body as a bug. Who knows? Perhaps it had something to do with her belief systems. With that one exception, she'd had the identical experience as I did.

To say that I was excited doesn't even come close to describing how I felt. Now there was absolutely no doubt of the validity of a secret place in the heart. This experience held such enormous human potential and could truly change the course of human history away from extinction. And what the Kogi Mamas wanted me to do was teach or transmit this ability to other people. Why? Because as guardians of the balance of the world, the Kogi Mamas believe that if we remember what and who is in our hearts, we will no longer be able to kill the Earth with our unconscious technology. I believe they are right.

❤   ❤   ❤

For the next two weeks, the Kogi Mamas appeared in my dreams every night, all night long. They continued to teach me and reveal aspects of themselves that they thought I should know. It was clear, very clear, from these dreams that they wanted me to reveal this information to the technological cultures of the world.

Eventually I did have a personal meeting with the Kogi. But I learned nothing that they had not already taught me. They did, however, make suggestions, and I am using some of their advice to teach what I learned, but some of their advice I can't use. For example, the Kogi Mamas said that if I had students stand up in a completely dark room without sleep or food for nine days and nights, they would be able to enter the sacred space of the heart. This may be true, but it would not work in the modern world. Using my personal experience as a guide, I eventually found two ways that work as substitutes, which I will share with you before this book is over.

Chapter Four

The Sacred Space of the Heart

The sacred space of the heart, sometimes referred to as the secret chamber of the heart, is a timeless dimension of consciousness where all things are possible, here and now. Throughout the world's ancient writings and oral traditions are references to a secret or special place within the heart. The short verse from the Chandogya Upanishad at the beginning of this book is one example. Another is the book associated with the Torah called the "Secret Chamber of the Heart."

And perhaps science is now beginning to cautiously approach this very understanding. One research group, the Institute of HeartMath in Boulder Creek, California, which is connected with Stanford University, has found some very interesting new data. That information may be helpful to some of you trying to understand the heart. It's not an easy undertaking, but when the mind cooperates, the heart responds.

There has always been this paradox: when a baby is conceived, the human heart begins to beat before the brain is formed. This has led doctors to wonder where the intelligence to begin and regulate the heartbeat is coming from. To the surprise of the medical world, scientists at HeartMath have discovered that the heart has its own brain—yes, a real brain with actual brain cells. It is very small, has only about forty thousand cells, but it is a brain and obviously all that the heart needs. This was an enormous discovery and lends authenticity to those who for centuries have spoken of or written about the intelligence of the heart.

The scientists at HeartMath have made perhaps an even greater discovery about the heart. They have proven that the human heart generates the largest and most powerful energy field of any organ in the body, including the brain within the skull. They found that this electromagnetic field is about eight to ten feet in diameter, with the axis centered in the heart. Its shape resembles the donut form of a torus, which is often considered the most unique and primal shape in the universe.

Those who have studied both volumes of *The Ancient Secret of the Flower of Life* will find something very familiar about the heart's toroidal field. In Metatron's Cube you can find the five platonic solids within one another, and each one has a smaller replica of the original form contained within it—a cube within a cube, an octahedron within an octahedron and so forth.

Here, emerging from the secret space of the heart, is an electromagnetic toroidal field with a smaller toroidal field inside and both are centered on the same axis, just like the five platonic solids in Metatron's Cube.

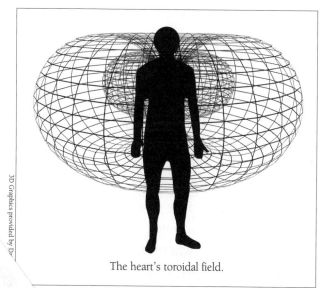

3D Graphics provided by Dr

The heart's toroidal field.

I have _____ d two very important aspects to this toroidal field. First, it can _____ d as a doorway to find and enter the secret chamber of the hear___ 'ructions on how to enter the secret place using this vortex can be ____ d later in this book. The second aspect has to do with the inner torus, the smaller one. This is not the place to explain how important this inner field is, but I will return to it when we talk about creating from the heart.

The sacred space of the heart is created in a fashion similar to the torus within the torus. There is the sacred space itself, but as you will see, within this sacred space is another, very small but very special space that is different and has unique applications.

Heart surgeons have learned another piece of information that could be related, but I am not sure of the significance. They have found that there is a tiny place in the heart that must never be touched for any reason or the person will immediately die, with no chance of reviving him or her. Whatever it is about this place, it certainly is important to life.

I am convinced that the toroidal electromagnetic field passes exactly through and is generated from the sacred space of the heart, but I am still not clear about the "brain of the heart" and "the place that cannot be touched or you die." If you understand or discover a relationship, please let me know.

Studying and Teaching Living in the Heart

Since late 1999, I have been studying and giving workshops on Living in the Heart. At the time of this writing, I have explored this experience with about four thousand people. I have learned so much and I continue to learn. I feel sure that there will be other parts to this book in the future, for we are now beginning to understand the images themselves that are generated by the heart.

The following is some of what I have learned, but first I would like to make a disclaimer. What I know at this point I have learned from direct experience and from the experiences of some of my students, and sometimes we don't understand what is going on for long periods of time. What I am about to say is what I believe to be true at this time and I may change my mind about some of this information. You must follow your own heart and be true to yourself. If something in this book does not work for you, just disregard it. I am certain that there is a way for you to find your sacred space of the heart.

In the first two years of giving the Living in the Heart workshop I found I could reach only about half of the participants; half of the people in each group completely "got it," whereas the point of the workshop went completely over the head (heart) of the other half. I finally began to mention before each workshop that this might happen, that about half the people would experience the sacred space within the heart and their lives would be changed by the experience, whereas the other half would go away not having experienced anything at all. Why is that so? I asked myself.

I have spent many hours contemplating this question. Based on the responses of hundreds of people who could not find the sacred space, it appears now that a major part of the reason lies in their emotional bodies. Those who experienced emotional trauma at some time in their lives feel the pain again when they enter the sacred space of the heart and want to leave immediately. This means that it might be necessary for you to clear emotional debris through therapy before you begin. Those who find a way to release their negative emotional energy, no matter how they do it, are able to enter the heart with little or no discomfort. Once in the heart—even if only for fifteen minutes—everything that had initially stopped them from entering the heart appears to dissolve and they have no problem returning to this sacred space.

Another problem I have encountered are the different ways people "see." Some see by using the inner facility of sight in the form of visions and dreams; others use sound and hearing to perceive the inner worlds; and still others use senses such as smell, taste and body sensations to see with. As a result, expectations as to how this experience is "supposed" to happen will sometimes get in the way. A short story will make this clear.

At the end of a recent workshop, a couple went home with one of them having entered the sacred space of the heart and the other one feeling like he had failed. (Even though I prepare people for this possibility, you can still feel discouraged when it is happening to you.) The husband, who felt that he had not had the experience, said to his wife, "I feel bad that nothing happened when I went into the meditation. I didn't see a thing. But I have to admit that the CD Drunvalo was playing, with the dolphins and whales, was incredible. The music was so good I could almost feel the water on my body." Astonished, his wife told him that I had not played a CD. In fact, there'd been no music at all. He could hardly believe her until he asked another person who'd been at the workshop as well and who confirmed that there'd been no music playing, no dolphin and whale sounds coming from a CD. This man was a musician, and this was his way of seeing. He had expected that he would see in a vision, but instead he saw with his ears.

We are now discovering that many people who thought they had not had an experience actually did have one, but because it didn't correspond with their expectations, they discounted the entire experience of having been in the heart space.

The Vibration of the Heart—The Easy Way Back

One of the first things I noticed when I entered my sacred space of the heart was the vibration that seemed to be coming from everywhere. This vibration obviously was not the heartbeat itself, since the sound was continuous—like the sound of Om, yet different. (Both times I found myself in the King's Chamber in the Great Pyramid in Egypt I experienced a vibration that seemed to be everywhere within the pyramid, even in the very stones I touched. I have talked with many other people who have experienced this same vibration there, and I believe it is almost exactly the vibration of the heart.)

When you enter the sacred space of the heart, one of the first things I would like you to do once you hear the vibration is to actually begin duplicating this inner sound with your physical voice. It doesn't have to be perfect, just as close as you can. This links the inner world of the heart with the outer world of the mind.

My wife has studied the ancient teachings on the way of the heart from Israel, from Madam Kolette of Jerusalem, which say this is always important—and I agree, after having witnessed so many people entering this space. What it does is ground the experience of the internal humming of the heart into this physical world, which then also presents another reason for doing this: a means of return.

Once you have experienced the sacred space of the heart and wish to return, you can simply tune to the heart vibration by humming the sound and, of course, moving out of the head into the heart. The vibration leads you directly to the sacred space of the heart and the return gets easier and easier. Eventually, this change from the mind to the heart can be accomplished in about two or three seconds.

My Personal Experience of the Sacred Space of the Heart

Before I begin, please understand that your experience and mine may be completely different and outwardly may even seem to have absolutely nothing in common. Though there are many correlations between any two people, like snowflakes, each person is unique. So please, don't set up expectations. The more you enter the heart like a child with open eyes and senses, the easier and more direct your experiences will be. I am telling you about other experiences simply so you can use them as a reference, not as a "law."

In the mid 1980s, I was meditating within the Mer-Ka-Ba, the human lightbody, and suddenly, quite unexpectedly, I found myself inside a cave carved out of solid stone that appeared to me to be totally real.

One end of the cave was rounded and domelike, with nothing in it except a circular area with a raised stone lip about twelve inches high and six feet in diameter and filled with pure, white silicone sand. Along the left wall of the main area were about twenty photographs of people, which appeared to be somehow embedded in the solid stone. I didn't recognize a single one of the people, nor did I understand why the photos were there. On the opposite wall was a crude opening about twelve feet wide and sixteen feet high. A wall of white light blocked the view of what was beyond the opening. I knew instinctively that whatever was behind this wall of light was something that was being hidden from myself by myself. I knew I had created this wall of light, but I had no idea why.

My cave.

As I "walked" around in this cave, everything felt familiar and at the same time it seemed like I was there for the first time. At the far end of the cave a staircase was carved out of the solid stone, winding around and down to another level. On this new level was a green light that left no shadow; it simply seemed to come from the air itself. I saw many sealed rooms—I believe there were hundreds of them. My inner guidance let me know that this part of the cave was for a later time in my life, so I went back to the main room.

I kept returning to the cave in my meditations, even though I wasn't trying to make it happen. About every two weeks or so I would find myself back in this space. Nothing ever changed nor did I ever discover anything new, until perhaps a year after I'd first discovered the cave.

I was sitting cross-legged in the round silicon sand area facing the solid rock wall (I'd found that once I entered this space, I often couldn't get out until the meditation was naturally over, so I got used to going to the ring and sitting in the sand because it somehow felt very good to sit there.) when I became aware of this awesome vibration that, once I felt it, was everywhere. However, as soon as I stepped out of the ring, the vibration dropped in pitch. Over time it became clear that this vibration was the same everywhere in the cave, except in the ring with the silicone sand. The change in pitch was the first indication that the sand area was unique to this space within my meditation, and I had always been attracted to the ring, where I would meditate for hours. But truly, at that time I had no idea what all this meant.

One day as I was yet again meditating inside the ring facing the stonewall, I noticed that the wall had started to become transparent. To my great surprise, when I touched the wall in the transparent area, my hand went right through the stone. Excitedly, I leaned forward out of the ring and pushed my hand as far as possible into the rock. My whole body kind of fell through the wall, and I found myself outside the cave, on the surface of a planet, deep inside a crevice on the side of a very high mountain.

I climbed out of the crevice so that I could take a look around. It was nighttime, and I saw the heavens filled with the familiar stars. But I couldn't see any life forms anywhere, only rock; I couldn't even find any dirt. After a few minutes I climbed back into the crevice and attempted to return to the inside of my cave, but at first I couldn't. There was a wall of solid rock. I didn't know what to do. I remember I actually felt fear for a moment.

I stood before the seemingly impenetrable rock wall for a while, and then I remembered the vibration of the sand ring. As soon as I began to make the sound and the sound went through my body, the rock wall began to become transparent so I could walk through it and return to the sand ring in the cave. Every time I did this, I could hardly believe it was actually happening, since everything appeared so very real.

After I'd discovered this trick, for about a year I would pass through the rock wall to the outside and then go for long walks to explore. This reality was just as real as my ordinary reality here on Earth—at least, I couldn't tell any difference. I could feel myself breathing; if I touched a rock, it felt the same as if I touched one in the regular world. Everything was exactly the same—except for this vibration that never stopped and the light that gave no shadow.

During that time in my life, I was living with a Native American family on the high desert plains outside of Taos, New Mexico. My home comprised an old 1957 Chevrolet school bus and a white, traditional Native American tipi that was nestled beside the bus. For about two and a half years, my life centered around this simple homestead.

One dark night, during a bitter cold snowstorm, there was a knock on the door of the bus. I was amazed that anyone was at my door because this was a full-blown, raging blizzard outside, and I was more than a mile from the nearest paved road. A young girl about twenty years old stood there freezing and asking for shelter, and of course I invited her inside.

Once she took off her hood so I could fully see her face, I had a shivering sense of déjà vu. But I couldn't immediately pinpoint where I had seen her before, so I began to ask her about possible places where we might have met. Then it hit me. She was in the first photo on the wall of my cave! At the first opportunity, I went into meditation to my cave and sure enough, her picture was right there on the wall. She stayed with me for about a year and had a huge influence on my life with the spiritual understandings that she presented to me.

Over the years, one by one the people in the photos on the wall entered my life with information and experiences that were—and still are—invaluable to me. However, at the time I met this young woman, I had no clue what the cave was or why I kept going there when I meditated. All I knew was that this cave was somehow extremely important to my reason for being on Earth.

Going Home

The sixteen-foot-high opening with the wall of light never changed over the years, that is, it didn't until January of 2002. I was in Germany giving a Living in the Heart workshop, and the group had just entered the sacred space of the heart for the first time. I'd also entered my sacred space of the heart and, as usual, found myself inside my cave. By now I understood that this was inside my heart space, but as I walked toward the wall of light, for the first time ever the opaque light concealing the opening was slightly transparent. I became excited, for this had never happened before, and I wondered what was going to come next.

We came out of our sacred spaces, and I dismissed the group for a short break of about a half hour. I started back to my room, when a woman approached me and said she had a gift for me.

She told me how she was walking on a beach in Greece, not thinking of anything but the beautiful place where she was, when she looked down at the sand and saw this most unusual rock. She picked it up and immediately the rock said to her, "Bring me to Drunvalo." And that was exactly what she did. She had wrapped it in a piece of cloth so I couldn't actually see the rock as she handed it to me. I thanked her and took it back to my room. When I unwrapped the rock, I was startled. I had never seen anything like it, not even close; it felt alien.

The rock.

The first thing I did was sit down to meditate holding the rock to my third eye. Without any predetermined thought, I found myself in front of the wall of light in my inner cave. Within a short time, the wall of light completely disappeared, and I could now see into the opening that had held my curiosity for so many years.

There, in their full beauty, were the heavens. Directly in the center of the opening was the Orion constellation, prominently displaying the three stars of the belt. Suddenly a brilliant, spiraling, golden beam of light came from the region around the center star of the Belt of Orion and expanded quickly until it encompassed my very body.

In that moment I remembered everything my Father had told me when I left the 13th dimension on how my spirit should move to find my way to Earth. Only, now I remembered how to move to find my way back home again! I was both happy—happy to remember so much that I had purposely forgotten—and apprehensive. Did this mean that I was about to leave Earth and go home? One of my angels appeared immediately to assure me that I wasn't leaving but that the vortex, "the spiraling, golden beam of light," had opened another form of communication for me that would be used in the future and would be paramount in my life. Remembering the movement of Spirit was important for another reason I would soon understand.

I left the meditation still holding this most unusual rock to my forehead and began to cry. The emotions I experienced about being reconnected to my Father in this way were such a release.

As I returned from the break and was about to begin teaching again, the same young woman came running to catch me before I started: "I forgot, when I gave you the rock I didn't give you the whole message from the rock. It said, 'Give me to Drunvalo. I am so he will remember how to go home.'" I had no words and instead hugged her to thank her from the bottom of my heart. Life truly is amazing!

In retrospect, I didn't fully become aware that the cave I entered during my Mer-Ka-Ba meditation was related to the sacred space of the heart until I encountered the Kogi of Colombia. They were the ones who illuminated this relationship, for which I will be eternally grateful.

What Is Time?

Now the magic really began . . .. During another Living in the Heart workshop in 2002, I was in meditation and entered the sacred space. As usual, I walked over to my special space to sit in the sand and meditate within my meditation when I saw that the ring was filled up to the brim with water, like a bathtub. I could also see that water had been overflowing and was running across the cave's floor to a place at the other side of the round area, where it was disappearing into a space between the floor and the wall.

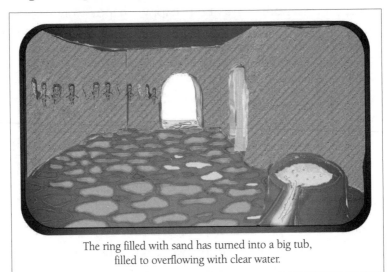

The ring filled with sand has turned into a big tub,
filled to overflowing with clear water.

Seeing this gave me the funniest feeling. I hadn't expected it and was bewildered, so I just stood there looking at the water, not knowing what to do or why this was happening. Suddenly a wave of water began to rise about a foot or two above the rim, spilling over it and flowing like a river toward the wall where the opening in the floor enlarged to receive the abundant water.

The amount of water kept increasing until it presented a truly alarming display. I had no idea what to do, so for quite a while I just stood next to what was now a cascading water fountain, thinking to myself, "My God, what is happening?" I just stood there in my meditation not knowing what to do. Finally, I simply left the meditation, a little bewildered.

The next day, during class, I entered my heart again to have an experience that would alter my meditational life forever. The flow of water continued, but it seemed to have calmed down to a continuous yet still heavy flow. The lip or rim of the stone circle had grown and was about three feet high, creating something more like a hot tub.

I wanted to enter my inner sacred space but kept standing there, contemplating if this was something I should—or should not—do. Finally, I felt I should just go ahead and do as I'd always done, so I climbed into the tub filled with swirling water. The water was cool but comfortable, about room temperature, and extremely pure and transparent. With the water flowing all around me, I soon began meditating, my eyes open and watching the rock wall in front of me. The wall slowly began to become transparent as I had seen so many times before, and I followed the overpowering urge to step through the wall.

As I climbed out of the familiar rock crevice to where I could see the barren planet, I was stopped in my tracks by the spectacle I was beholding. This "imaginary" planet was no longer barren! Everywhere, as far as I could see, there was abundant plant life; a virtual jungle stretched out before me in all directions, all the way to the horizon. How could this be?

No sooner had I finished the thought, when the image of the flowing water from my inner sacred space appeared, and I realized that this water had given life to the planet. But the plants were so mature! Could it be that time in this world was not what I thought it was? I had so many questions.

After a long time of contemplation and awe, I returned to my inner sacred space and reentered my body. Once I was back in this world, I spent days pondering the meaning of my latest experience. Really, what did this represent? My inner guidance, the angels, just silently stood by, leaving me to find my own conclusions.

Others' Sacred Spaces—Some Examples

I have listened to over one thousand people telling the stories of their experiences within their hearts. Even though there are some similarities, it is clear that the images of the heart are more like dreams than this fixed, structured reality in which we all live.

The nature of people's experiences covers a wide spectrum. Be careful with any predetermined expectations. Be childlike, with an open heart as you enter your inner space. Your experience will almost certainly be unique to only you. Here are some examples of what other people experienced so you can get an idea how diverse our sacred spaces of the heart are.

"When I asked that my sacred space be filled with light, it happened instantly. I was so happy when it happened, because usually nothing happens when I ask for something. It was a soft, glowing light—not a bright light like in my home. I looked around and discovered I was in a large, elaborate Egyptian-looking temple. Only—the stones seemed to be electric and emitting light, too. There were hieroglyphs on the walls, and as I moved closer to see them better they began to dance like they were alive. Somehow, one line of about twenty images made complete sense to me. I can't tell you what it said, I just knew the meaning in my heart, and I began to cry."

"I turned away and saw a doorway, very high. I passed through the door into another room, where there was this beautiful, regal woman with dark hair, dark eyes and a long, golden robe. She looked Egyptian. She took my hand without saying a word and led me to a small, simple room; she ushered me in and disappeared. I knew instantly that I had just entered my inner sacred space; I was certain."

"Suddenly the room began to change shape and it kept growing in size until it was over a mile across; it kept growing until the walls disappeared. And then I realized I was in deep space. Then you [Drunvalo] asked us to return."

A young man, who said he didn't think anything would happen with him because "It never does," shared his experience:

"When I asked there to be light, nothing happened. So I began to see if I could sense my way around like you [Drunvalo] had suggested. Somehow I knew where I was; everything was very familiar. I turned to my left and, almost like an impressionistic painting, I could see faint outlines of something that appeared to be nearby.

"I slowly began to make out forms and shapes, and the shapes soon became brighter until I was in a world of just light—meaning it wasn't solid but more like a hologram. The light began to move, forming geometric patterns. I felt myself moving, too, following one of the streaming flows of light back to its source. The beauty was intense and the sense of moving very fast was exhilarating. It, whatever it was, kept pulling me, and I could see it. Lines of light were coming from all over the universe back to this one place I was quickly approaching. By now the size and grandeur of this event were on a galactic scale. I felt like a tiny speck in all of this.

"As I flowed like mercury into the center of this light field, I knew I was Home—with a capital letter! I had been there before. At the center of this awesome experience was a round ball of living water. I slipped into the middle of this ball of light-filled water just when you asked us to return. I know I will go back there. I didn't want the experience to stop. I didn't want to return. I was so alive."

The stories go on and on—always different, always intimately personal to the meditator of the heart. After listening to hundreds of these stories, it becomes clear that there is another reality in the heart that is just as important and perhaps more primal than this structured world of the mind in which we all seemingly live.

What Can Stop You from Having This Experience

There are reasons why some people cannot enter the heart or, if they do find this special place, they feel compelled to leave immediately. It took me almost two years of teaching and listening to those who could not enter before I began to understand why this is so.

As I touched on before, those who have had traumatic emotional experiences in their lives, especially negative experiences around relationships and love, often relive their pain when they enter the sacred space of the heart, and it is so painful that they feel they must leave. This is the most prevalent problem.

There is also the problem of fear—the fear of the unknown. Some people realize instantly how "real" the images of the heart are when they begin to experience them, and fear enters their spirit and drives them away. I have found that if this is the case and if one can get the person to stay just for a little while, the fear will often go away and all is well. The secret is how to get someone to stay long enough for the fear to dissolve.

The third problem, which I also touched on earlier in the book, is when people have expectations of being able to "see" in a certain manner and don't realize that they can "see" in other ways—by hearing, touching, smelling or tasting.

As I mentioned, in the beginning I could reach only about 50 percent of the audience. But by January of 2002, I had learned about these issues that could keep people away from their sacred spaces of the heart. At the workshop in Germany, 174 out of 180 people were able to experience their inner sacred space of the heart, yet we are still learning or remembering.

Chapter Five

The Unity of Heaven
and Earth

One thing that indigenous peoples of the world have taught me is that before any important ceremony, one must connect in love with Mother Earth, then with Father Sky and through this experience ultimately with Great Spirit, or God. It is no different when one is about to enter the sacred space of the heart, otherwise this space will remain elusive.

I had originally learned what I am about to tell you in 1981 from one of my Taos Pueblo mentors, Jimmy Reyna, and knew it in a very simple and unrefined manner. But here enters one of the great spiritual teachers of the Kriya yoga traditions, speaking in elegant terms.

I was about to go on stage during an event called "The Solar Heart" on Jekyll Island, Georgia, in about 1994. Several spiritual teachers were taking turns to lead the audience into a higher and higher unity with Spirit. I was to be next. I was behind the stage in a small back room sitting before a meditation altar where someone had placed a single lit candle and a set of photographs from the Self-Realization Fellowship. There were pictures of Krishna, Jesus, Babaji, Lahiri Maharshi, Sri Yukteswar and Yogananda. I knew that before I had to actually go on stage someone would come and get me, and I already knew what I was going to speak about, so there was nothing left to do but to center. For me there is no better way to do this than to enter into meditation.

I acknowledged the teachers for the greatness they are and closed my eyes to begin meditating. Slowly the world around me began to fade into the distance, and as the energy began to increase, I had a vision. This single moment altered the course of that evening with the audience and later the course of almost everything in my spiritual world.

In a short time, Sri Yukteswar appeared to me with this noble expression on his face. Though I have had a close relationship with Yogananda, Sri Yukteswar's disciple, I have never really thought about Sri Yukteswar himself. But there he was.

Sri Yukteswar.

The Unity Breath

Sri Yukteswar went directly to the point, as I will now. He told me that in India no one would even consider approaching the divine without a certain state of mind and heart, and he gave me very specific instructions on exactly how to consciously connect to the divine and finally with God. Here is what he told me.

"You can be anywhere, but for me, I use an altar with a single candle to focus my mental attention. I feel and know the presence of my teachers, and we all begin to breathe together, as one."

Unify with the Divine Mother

"Let your attention shift to a place on Earth that you feel is the most beautiful place in the world. It could be anywhere—a mountain scene with trees, lakes and rivers; or an arid, sandy desert with almost no life—whatever you perceive as beautiful. See as much detail as you can.

"For example, if your place is a mountain scene, see the mountains and the white, billowing clouds. See and sense the forest and the trees moving with the wind. See the animals—the deer and elk, little rabbits and squirrels. Look down and see the clear water of the rivers. Begin to feel love for this place and for all of nature. Continue to grow into this space of love with nature until your heart is beating with the warmth of your love.

"When the time feels right, send your love to the center of the Earth using your intention so that Mother Earth can directly feel the love you have for her. You can place your love into a small sphere to contain it and send it to the Mother if you wish, but it is your intention that is so important. Then wait, as a child. Wait until Mother Earth sends her love back to you and you can feel it. You are her child, and I know she loves you.

"As your Mother's love enters your body, open completely, allowing this love to move anywhere throughout your body. Let it enter all of your cells. Let it move throughout your lightbody. Let it move wherever it wishes to move. Feel this beautiful love your Mother has surrounded you with and remain in this union with Mother Earth until it feels complete."

Unify with the Divine Father

"At the right moment, which only you can know, without breaking the love union with your Mother, look to your Father, to your Heavenly Father. Look to the rest of creation beyond the Earth. Place your attention on a night sky. See the Milky Way as it meanders across the heavens. Watch the planets and the Moon swirl around you and the Earth. Feel the Sun hidden beneath the Earth. Realize the incredible depth of space.

"Feel the love you have for the Father, for the Divine Father is the spirit of all of creation, except the Divine Mother. And when this love becomes so great that it just can't stay inside you any longer, let it move into the heavens with your intention. Again, you can send your love into the heavens inside a small sphere, if you wish."

Sri Yukteswar says to place your love in a small sphere and with your intention send it into the heavens. He says to send it to the unity consciousness grid around the Earth. If you don't know what this grid is, then don't worry, just do as most of the indigenous peoples of the world do: send your love to the Sun. Like the grids, the Sun is connected to all the other suns or stars and eventually to all life everywhere. Some people, such as the Hopi of the Southwest of the United States, send their love to the Great Central Sun, which is another concept that not everyone has but that is equally valid. Choose one—which one doesn't matter. The intent is for your love to reach all life everywhere.

Sri Yukteswar continued: *"Once your love has been sent into the heavens to the Divine Father, again you wait; you wait for the Father to send his love back to you. And of course, he will always do so. You are his child forever, and the Divine Father will always, always love you. And just like with the Mother's love, when you feel the love of the Divine Father enter your being, let it move anywhere it wants to. It is your Father's love, and it is pure."*

The Holy Trinity Is Alive

"At this moment something that rarely happens is manifesting: the Holy Trinity is alive on Earth. The Divine Mother and the Divine Father are joined with you in pure love and you, the Divine Child, complete the triangle."

According to Sri Yukteswar, it is only in this particular state of consciousness that God can be known directly. And so the final step in this meditation is to become aware of the presence of God—all around you and within you.

For this part of the meditation, Sri Yukteswar originally gave me a very complex way of being aware of God, but after speaking with many elders of various tribes around the world, I feel we can simplify the way to reach this final state of consciousness. It really is simple: Once you are in the Holy Trinity, you can achieve this experience by simply opening your heart to the presence of God. For some reason that only God knows, in the Holy Trinity state the presence of God is easily perceivable.

Sri Yukteswar gave me the name of this meditation: the Unity Breath. God is always everywhere, but humans do not always perceive God. The Unity Breath meditation takes you directly, consciously into God's presence.

For some this state of consciousness is all that is necessary to complete all cycles created by life, or in another way of saying it, it is the doorway to approach all the sacred ceremonies of life, such as our birth into this world, sacred marriage and even death. According to the Native Americans, even the ceremonies of planting and harvesting crops require this particular connection to Great Spirit for the crops to grow and be healthy.

The natural way is to cocreate with God, or Great Spirit, to assist in the cycles of nature to bring balance to life. According to the Bible we are the keepers of the Garden (or nature) as described in the story of Adam and Eve, and in this modern time we still are, but we have forgotten our purpose. Without this inner connection with God we are separate and lost, hence this meditation of Sri Yukteswar is the opening to remember God and to enter and remember the sacred space of the heart.

Going on Stage

At this point, Sri Yukteswar became very stern. He looked me straight in the eyes and said, *"Drunvalo, I want you to go out onto the stage today and teach the audience this meditation I just taught you."* He looked at me like he really meant it, and I thought I'd better not disobey him. Then he bowed and disappeared.

I remember hearing the knock on the door that told me that it was my turn. I remember getting up, confused. I didn't know what to do. I'd had a plan as to what I was going to do and say, but this seemed to override everything. I told the stagehand that I would come along in just one minute, closed the door and quickly brought in the angels. They advised me to do as told by Sri Yukteswar, that eventually I would understand. And so I did, and so eventually I did understand.

Once I was out in front of the audience I told them what had just happened and that we were about to enter into a meditational state that Sri Yukteswar had strongly suggested we all experience. I led the audience through the steps while I followed my own words. Then there was silence, and bliss.

A long time later I was pulled out of the meditation by a young man tugging at my sleeve and telling me that we should be ready to go to lunch in ten minutes. Everyone in the room, except those watching over the group, was deep in meditation. I asked people to slowly return, but for the first time in my life I found many in the audience who were so deep into the meditation that they couldn't or didn't want to come out of it.

After several attempts to retrieve everybody, there were still about thirty people who just did not want to return. We sent people to them individually to get them out of their meditation, and all of them eventually did come out—except one young man who we thought was going to have to be taken to a hospital. After maybe twenty more minutes, while everybody else was eating lunch, he finally opened his eyes.

All I could think was, "What happened?" I'd had an experience that stayed with me beyond the meditation. I could still feel the love of my Mother and Father and the presence of God everywhere and in everything. It was delicious. It was beautiful.

Over the years I have learned to be careful with the Unity Breath meditation. Once one enters this state, one does not want to leave prematurely; it feels too good. So if you practice this meditation, leave ample time for yourself. Shut off the phones and do what is necessary to remain undisturbed with no time limit. Let the experience unfold like a summer flower.

It Is So Simple

Now that you know the Unity Breath, always enter this state of consciousness first before you enter the sacred space of the heart.

Otherwise, no matter how hard you try to find the sacred space, it will run from you; it will hide, leaving no trace.

Once you have reached the level of consciousness achieved by the Unity Breath, you may find that it gets easier and easier until, finally, you are in this place all the time. This is the ideal according to all of my mentors who know of this meditation.

I believe that the Unity Breath creates the vibration within you that allows you to find the holy grail, the sacred space of the heart, the place where God originally created all that is. It is so simple. What you have always been looking for is right inside your own heart.

Chapter Six

Leaving the Mind and Entering the Heart

First Exercise—Moving around the Body

Second Exercise—Entering the Heart

Third Exercise—The Head "Om" and the Heart "Aah"

Two Ways into the Sacred Space of the Heart

The Unity Breath is the prerequisite to entering the sacred space of the heart. However, there are still two main obstacles to actually entering this sacred space.

First, for the Western consciousness the Unity Breath alone is not enough to find where the secret sacred space of the heart is. Why? Because your mind will always create an illusion to lead you away from the truth; your mind will always say to you, "Don't listen to your heart. Only I know Source. Follow me and my logic and everything will be perfect. My science is the only way to know the truth." Using the thinking process and logic, the mind will keep you inside your head. And as long as you remain inside your head, inside your skull, you will never, ever find the sacred space of the heart. The mind has hidden the power of the heart from many for thousands of years.

Second, one must know about the mobility of spirit within the human body. Without this knowledge, no amount of effort to reach the sacred space of the heart can produce results. One needs to discover that spirit can move within the body and then literally leave the location of the head and mind to enter into the completely altered state of consciousness and intelligence that is found within the heart.

From personal experience and from the experience of thousands of people, I have discovered that overcoming the human thought process is a very easy thing to do once it becomes clear what it is one must do. If you just sit there and listen and/or respond to your thoughts, you remain trapped in the head, and your thoughts will continue perpetually and will stop you.

There are a few systems of meditation that help you overcome, or bypass, the mind, such as the Vipassana meditation where one sits in meditation for many hours until the stillpoint is achieved. But there is a simpler way, and that is for spirit to simply leave the head and the mind altogether. And for entering the sacred space of the heart, it is the only way I am aware of.

Seldom have I found anyone who knows that the human spirit can move around inside the human body. Most people look at me like I am crazy when I talk about this. Most indigenous peoples, however, completely understand; in their spiritual processes they experience exactly that.

The human spirit is separate from the body. When we die, we (our spirit) leave the body and return to a world that appears separate from this one. The human body is like a coat—we put it on to be human and take it off to be something else. In my studies I have found that at this time in history the human spirit is usually focused in the pineal gland, in the center of the head. Spirit being located in the pineal gland means experiencing the human body from the point of view of looking at the world through the eyes and feeling like the outer world is separate from oneself.

It seems like we are directly behind the eyes, even though we can experience other parts of our bodies. Now, most of us have had the experience of placing our attention in other parts of the body—a hand or foot, for example—but we still do this with the spirit being located in the pineal gland.

There are other ways of experiencing the human body, and it is one of these other ways that I wish to teach you now. You must understand and experience this part before you can continue to find the sacred space of the heart.

First Exercise—Moving around the Body

It's easiest to do this first exercise if you think of it as a game—and even easier if you look at yourself as a child. Don't take this seriously; seriousness, which comes from the mind, will only interfere with the outcome of this exercise. Just have fun! For it is your childlike nature that will allow you to easily enter the heart—not the adult, calculating thought processes of your mind.

● Place your attention on your right hand. Feel around inside your hand and "be" there as much as you can. Is your spirit still in your head, sensing your hand? This would be the normal way. (I'm having you do this because this is *not* what I am talking about; focusing on your hand is remaining within the head.)

● Think of your spirit, you, as something separate from your body. See your spirit as perhaps a very small sphere of light, about the size of a marble.

In the next step we are going to move out of the head, in the form of a tiny sphere of light, into the throat chakra. First let's have an intellectual discussion to prepare the mind.

Think of a tall building with an elevator mounted on the outside. The elevator is completely made of glass so that you can see outside while you're in it; you can see the entire building as you travel from the top all the way down to the ground. On your way down you can see the top of the building seemingly move away from you. Your relative position changes and you actually see the building from a different location, right?

● Now close your eyes (this is important) and use only your imagination to see with. "See" yourself as a little round sphere of light moving out of the pineal gland or head area and down, just like an elevator, to the throat chakra.

As you move out of the head, you will see, in your imagination, your physical head moving away from you, just like the top of the building. Don't think about this process—that will definitely interfere with what you are doing. Just play the game.

● Once you reach the throat chakra, you will see, or sense, in your inner vision your head way above you, and it will seem like you are looking out of your throat. Be aware of the softness of the throat all around you. You will seem to be at about the same level as your shoulders. You can do this!

If you can't do it at first, then stop, relax and remember to play this exercise like a game. Keep doing it until, with your inner vision, you can see or sense yourself, your spirit moving out of your head and into your throat.

● Return to your head. With your inner vision, you will see or sense your body moving down while your spirit approaches the inside of the head, or skull.

Once you enter the head again, be sure you are facing the right direction, toward your eyes. (You might think this sounds funny or is a given, but some people have actually returned into their heads facing the wrong way, and it disoriented them. This probably will not happen to you, but if it does, simply turn toward your eyes and everything will right itself very quickly.)

● Now leave your head and move down to the throat again. Once you arrive there, be aware of the soft tissue around the throat.

● Return again to the head, seeing the change in your inner vision. Once in your head, this time be aware of the hard, solid bone of the skull surrounding you. Feel the difference.

● Again, move back down to the throat and be aware of the soft tissue surrounding you. Feel the difference.

● This time we will go farther. Move from your throat over to your right shoulder. In your inner vision, assuming you are still facing toward the front of your body, notice how the head is offset toward the left. Feel the bones of your shoulder.

● Now continue down the arm to the right hand and enter the palm area of your hand. See the fingers all around you. Often they will seem to be very big, since at this moment you are very small. Feel the fingers all around you.

● Return to the shoulder, then back to the throat. Always stop at the throat as a reference point before you enter back into the head. Now move on back into the head, making sure you are facing forward, toward your eyes. Feel the hardness of the skull all around you.

You have completed the first exercise. You can continue, if you wish, to practice moving to different parts of your body. Leave your heart alone at this point, but you can go anywhere else you choose. It is your body. Always return to the throat and stop long enough to orient yourself before reentering the head.

Second Exercise—Entering the Heart

At this point we are ready to enter the heart, but we are not going to move to the sacred space of the heart quite yet. First you need to feel the difference between the head and the heart.

- Begin as you have just learned, by closing your eyes and moving out of your head down to your throat.

- Wait until you feel right, and then move toward your physical heart, not the heart chakra(s). Sense or see in your inner vision your heart and feel yourself moving toward it. When you reach the heart, continue and move right through the membrane into the heart itself.

- Hear and feel the heart beating. Feel the softness of the tissue surrounding you. Feel how different this is from the hardness of the skull around the head. The heart is female and the head is male. It is so obvious.

- Although you could stay here as long as you wish, it's probably best to linger no more than five minutes. Don't be concerned with the Sacred Space at this time. Only feel what it feels like to be in the heart.

- When the time seems right, move out of the heart, through the membrane and continue over to the throat. Stop for a moment to feel the throat and then continue back up to the head. Make sure you are correctly aligned with your eyes.

- Feel what it's like to be back in the head again and compare it with being in the heart. Feel the hardness of the skull and compare it with the softness of the heart tissue.

You have finished the second exercise.

Third Exercise—The Head "Om" and the Heart "Aah"

We are now going to do the last exercise three times back to back. When you are in your head, chant the sound of "Om," and when you are in your heart, chant the sound of "Aah." To be clear, I am asking you to use your voice to make these sounds at the appropriate place. This exercise is subtle, but it really helps to understand, in your cells, everything you've done up to this point.

◎ Begin by closing your eyes and feeling the hard skull around you. Make the sound of "Om" one time with your voice. As you make this sound, feel how it resonates within your skull. Feel it.

◎ Now move down to your throat and stop there for a moment. Then move over to your heart, seeing in your inner vision the heart approaching. Enter the heart and feel the space.

◎ Make the sound of "Aah" one time and feel how this sound resonates within the softness of the heart. Again, feel it.

◎ Leave the heart and move to the throat. Wait a moment, then continue on to the head. Feel the hardness of the skull and make the sound of "Om."

◎ Repeat these steps two more times and then just sit and feel how the two places are so very different—as different as male is to female.

You have completed the third exercise.

Two Ways into the Sacred Space of the Heart

When the Kogi of South America taught me, they pointed out that the best way to enter the sacred space of the heart was by standing in a completely dark room or space, with eyes closed, without eating any food, without drinking any water and without any sleep—for nine days and nine nights. They said that by doing this, Mother Earth would come and the way would be shown.

Their way of life allows for such a meditation, but for us this would be an enormous abyss to cross. The Kogi, who understand the technological society very little, asked me to teach entering the sacred space of the heart this way, but I knew it would present a real problem. I told them that such a nine-day meditation would be impossible for almost everyone in the modern world. There might be a few people who could do it, but if they wanted to reach the world, we would have to find another way.

So I asked my inner guidance, and slowly two other ways were uncovered. I feel sure that there are more ways to enter the sacred space of the heart, but these two ways do work. It doesn't really matter how you find your way in, and as long as your heart is pure, you will be able to stay.

Entering the sacred space of the heart does not involve a learning process; rather, it is a remembering process, for we have always been in this space, from the beginning. We have chosen to divert our attention to this way of polarity consciousness, but once we've learned the lesson, I feel certain that we will return to the primal state of oneness.

The first way I tried was based on the HeartMath Institute's discovery of the toroidal field around the heart—in particular, the discovery of the small torus within the larger torus. The premise was that the actual source of this enormous electromagnetic field was within the sacred space of the heart. Therefore, if one was to track back along the geometric energy lines of this field, they would take one directly into this holy space. And what I found is that this is true—they do.

This first method is male in nature, meaning that it can be communicated to someone else, and if that person does exactly what is conveyed, the result will always be the same. Unfortunately, male methods don't work on females very well. The second method, female in nature, is so simple that it took me quite a while to see it.

In the following chapter, we will put all the instructions together into one complete method to reach the sacred space of the heart. For now you only need to mentally understand what is being asked. The actual experience will come soon—we will come to the place where the physical heart is in front of us, and at that moment we will see or sense or feel the toroidal field with our inner vision as it sits around the heart, and we will focus on the inner, smaller torus.

The Male Way into the Heart

Here is the male way in: As you move toward the heart and see the smaller toroidal field, rise up above the field until you see the torus from above. This energy field is a vortex, as I explained before, moving around and around like water going down a drain. It moves slower along the outer edge and gets faster and faster toward the center, then it falls through the center—again just like water going down the drain. For some people the vortex moves clockwise and for others it moves counterclockwise. The direction in which it is rotating might be related to sexual preference and does not seem to matter.

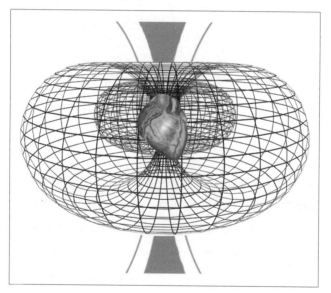

For this meditation, when you see the top of the toroidal field, see or feel which way it is moving. Then, like a leaf floating on a river, let your spirit rest on the spiraling energy.

Begin to experience yourself going around and around—slowly at first, but as you get closer to the center you begin to move faster and faster until finally you enter the center and begin to fall. There is nothing to fear. Just let yourself go, and fall. In a moment you will realize that everything is very, very still. Like being in the eye of the hurricane, you are now inside the sacred space of the heart. You are really there.

The Female Way into the Heart

Here is the female way in: As I mentioned, this way is so simple that I couldn't see it at first. The instructions are easy, and the experience will be different for each of you when you use this method. It is not important whether your body is male or female, but if following your heart is your way, then this way is for you.

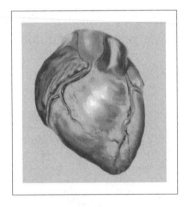

For the female way in, all you do is see, sense or feel yourself approaching the heart and then allow yourself to enter its membrane, just like you did earlier. Except this time let your female psychic nature take over and let your intuition lead you to the sacred space of the heart. Then let go and move, knowing you are in truth going to move straight into this holy place.

Try one way and if it doesn't work, then try the other way. Remember, you are a child of God. You know this place, for you and God have always been as one here. Always.

Chapter Seven

The Sacred Space of the Heart Meditation

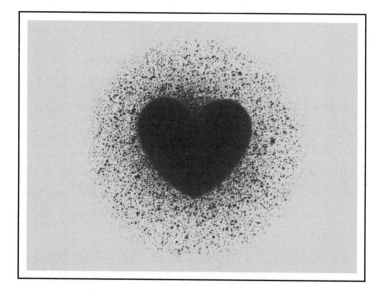

Preparing for the Meditation

The Unity Breath

Choose Your Way into the Heart

Exploring the Sacred Space of the Heart for the First Time

Returning to the Sacred Space of the Heart

It's now time for the real thing, for actually having the experience of your sacred space of the heart. If you choose, the words in this chapter will lead you into what thousands of people have experienced, the holy of holies—your own heart, the source of creation. (The following words are on the enclosed CD so that you do not have to read while you are in meditation.)

Don't have any expectations. Just be a kid and play with the possibilities. If your experience is real, you will soon know. Remember that Jesus said, ". . . except ye . . . become as little children, ye shall not enter into the kingdom of heaven."

Preparing for the Meditation

Find a place that is perfect for you to meditate in. Build a simple altar with a candle and fresh flowers. Choose a place where you will not be disturbed, as this will not only make it easier for you to meditate, but it will assure your successful return.

Use a pillow to support your spine if you are sitting on the floor. If you are in a chair, put your feet flat on the floor and keep your back straight. If you are standing, find your center of gravity and slightly sway or move, as your body wishes.

For this meditation, a very dark place is best—the darker the better. In fact, in the beginning even the candle could interfere with this meditation. Once you have done it several times, it is not as important any more that it is perfectly dark, since you will be able to enter this place just by closing your eyes. But in the beginning, dark is good. Even better is a "Mindfold" or other blindfold that completely blocks out all light; then it doesn't matter whether or not the room is perfectly dark.

Close your eyes and begin to breathe rhythmically, so that the length of time you are breathing in is the same as your breathing out. Breathe gently, comfortably. Follow your breathing pattern and let go of your thoughts of your world; forget your worries for a while.

Follow your breathing for a few minutes until you are relaxed and comfortable. There is no hurry. Where you are about to go, there is no time.

When everything feels right, shift your attention from your breathing to your inner vision and begin the Unity Breath meditation, the starting point for all sacred ceremonies.

The Unity Breath

For an expanded description of the Unity Breath meditation, go back to Chapter Five.

- See a place in nature that you feel is beautiful and visualize this place in as much detail as you can. If you are one who does not see but senses in other ways, then use the other ways to see; we all have our own way. Feel the love you have for nature and Mother Earth. Let this love grow in your heart until you feel it in your whole body.

- When the time feels right, take your love and put it into a small, round sphere, and with your intention send it down deep into the Earth, to the very center of the Earth. Let your Divine Mother know how much you love her. Let her feel your love. Then wait for Mother Earth to send her love back to you.

- When you feel this love from your Mother enter your energy body, just let it move in any way and any place. Just let it be. Feel the flow of love between you and the Earth. You can stay here as long as you wish.

- When the time seems right, without breaking the flow of love between you and your Divine Mother, shift your attention to your Divine Father. In your inner vision, see or sense a night sky, the Milky Way, the depths of space. See the planets and the Moon glowing in the night sky and feel the presence of the Sun hidden far beneath the Earth.

- Let yourself feel the love you have for all the rest of creation and your Divine Father. When the time feels right, put your love in a small sphere and send it into the heavens with the intention that it go directly to your Divine Father. Send it to the grids around the Earth, the Sun or the Great Central Sun. Let your Father know how you feel . . . and wait.

Wait for the love from your Divine Father to come to Earth and enter your body. When it does, let it move in any way and to any place. Don't try to control this love; just feel it.

● At this moment, the Holy Trinity is alive on Earth. The Divine Mother and the Divine Father and you, the Divine Child, are joined in pure love. It is a sacred moment in its own right, so just be with your divine parents and feel the love.

● From this place of pure love open to the awareness of the presence of God, who is all around you and who lives within you. Simply be aware of and feel this union of cosmic forces and breathe the breath of life.

Choose Your Way into the Heart

Choose which way you wish to enter the sacred space of the heart—using the male vortex of the toroidal field or the female path of your intuition only. It doesn't matter which method you choose; it is completely up to you.

○ With your intention and will power, leave the mind and move down into the throat. Feel the throat all around you and then move toward the physical heart.

If you choose the male toroidal pathway, rise up above the heart until your inner vision can see or sense the inner toroidal field, the vortex. Then, like a leaf on a river, let your spirit drift on the moving vortex, in whichever direction it is rotating. Feel yourself spiraling around and around until you fall into the center of the vortex. Continue to fall until you feel the stillness. You are now in the sacred space of the heart.

If you choose the female, intuitive pathway, see or sense the heart approaching and move right through the membrane of the heart into its interior. Once inside, turn your movements over to your intuition and let yourself be guided directly to the sacred space of the heart.

○ You are there.

The first thing you do is look around. If it is dark, which it very well might be, say in your inner world, "Let there be light," and watch or sense how the darkness turns into a world of light.

○ Once you can see or sense the sacred space of the heart, become aware of the vibration, the sound that permeates this place. Listen to this sound for a while. When the time seems right, begin to actually make the sound. Hum, making it sound as close as possible to what you hear with your inner hearing. Try to duplicate it. Keep the humming sound going with your voice and then begin to explore this holy space.

Exploring the Sacred Space of the Heart for the First Time

The adventure begins. Some will immediately remember that they have been there millions of times before, whereas others will feel that this is the first time. No matter what you experience, there are some things you should know.

The sacred space of the heart is older than creation itself. Before there were galaxies to live within, there was this space. All the places you have traveled within this creation you have recorded within this space. And so at first you might begin to remember what this is all about, what life is about.

Within this space, you have recorded your heart's deepest desire that you wish to manifest and live more than any other thing or event. It is there for you to remember, your purpose for coming to Earth in the first place—whether it was recently or in ancient times—the very reason for being here. You might begin to explore these recordings or you may wish to let your intuition lead you again. Eventually, all will be revealed to you as you yourself have set up the timing and the flow.

On your first journey into the sacred space of the heart, it may be best to limit the time you spend there to less than thirty minutes. You could use a timer or have somebody there who will bring you back at a given time. This sacred space is very seductive, and one needs experience to learn how long one should stay. Begin with a short time and let the time increase as you learn.

Returning to the Sacred Space of the Heart

It is when you enter the sacred space of the heart for the second time that you are to find the space within the space, what the Upanishad calls the tiny space within the heart. Earlier in the book I said that there is a small space within the sacred space of the heart that is extremely important. I ask you to find this place using your intuition when you enter the heart the second time. This place will change everything.

Entering the sacred space of the heart the second time is much easier and quicker. Eventually, as you practice, you will find that you will be able to get into your holy space in a matter of seconds.

● Simply close your eyes and confirm your love for Mother Earth and Father Sky by feeling the emotion of the love that connects you.

● Feel yourself leave the head and move to the throat. From there, move toward the heart and begin to hum the sound that you know is within the sacred space of your heart. The vibration of your humming will take you very quickly back to your sacred space—and you are there. It is so easy once you know the way.

○ With your intention, allow yourself to be guided to the small space within the sacred space of the heart. This space is different for each person, but for everyone it has similar qualities.

○ Once you know you have found this place of creation, move inside and become familiar with the way it feels.

Notice that the vibration goes up in pitch; notice that this small space feels completely different from any other place in the heart. This is where creation began. It may take you a while or you may realize immediately where you are: The Creator of all life resides within this space; within this space all things are possible.

● ● ●

Students have shown me that one of the easiest ways to see God is to ask the person you love the most to be with you in this inner space. If you have more than one person you love the most, then choose one. Have you seen the movie *Contact*? The advanced race presented itself to the earthling, who was exploring higher consciousness, as her father whom she loved more than anyone. This made it easiest for her to accept what was happening.

So invite the person you love the most, no matter whether he or she is alive or has passed to the other worlds, for in this place all hearts are intimately connected. Once this person appears in your inner space with you, there are no guidelines. Just let happen whatever happens, for God will know exactly what to do.

Each day return to your sacred space of the heart and continue to explore. It is your birthright to remember who you really are and why you are here on Earth. You are an incredible child of God having a dream that you are a human being on a tiny planet in the middle of nowhere. What happens when you remember who you really are? That is something only you can know.

Now you know your way *Home*. Within the sacred space of the heart, all worlds, all dimensions, all universes, all of creation found their birth. Interconnecting through your one heart are all the hearts of all life everywhere!

Chapter Eight

The Mer-Ka-Ba and the Sacred Space of the Heart

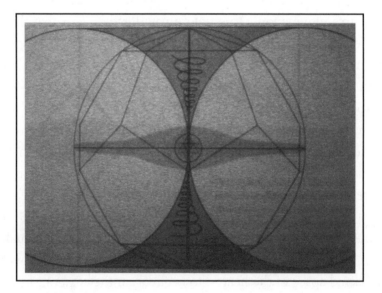

Combining the Sacred Space of the Heart with the Mer-Ka-Ba

The Angels Explain

Many students have been waiting for the next level of instructions for the human lightbody, the Mer-Ka-Ba. It has taken me almost nineteen years to get this information, since everything happens in its own time and in divine order.

There is still one more level, or part, but that is in the future and will come when God decides. At this point I have only part of the information for this third and final part. Once the three parts are combined and lived, true ascension can begin.

Many people have taken the Mer-Ka-Ba teaching from the two volumes of *The Ancient Secret of the Flower of Life*, have been to one of my workshops or have watched the FOL video series and have decided to teach this information. It is unfortunate for the Earth that this has happened. These people believe that the Mer-Ka-Ba is complete and that by changing it in some way it will take one to the "proper" level of consciousness. This is not true. No amount of knowledge of Mer-Ka-Ba science based only upon the energy forms will do this—no matter where or who it is coming from within the universe.

Melchizedek consciousness, which is older than all of this creation itself, has witnessed the beginning of the creation in this space/time/dimension universe, one of a multitude of universes. From this experience, Melchizedek tradition has realized that through living the three parts of the Mer-Ka-Ba the individualized spirit is always brought back to the conscious presence of God within the sacred space of the heart—to begin again the creation, in a new manner. And this is exactly what the Mer-Ka-Ba experience eventually leads to.

But before it can happen, spirit must remember the three parts, combine them into one and live the experience. In this chapter and the next, you will learn about the second part—combining the sacred space of the heart with the human Mer-Ka-Ba field.

If you have not learned the Mer-Ka-Ba meditation, it is fine to remember only within the sacred space of the heart. Eventually, it will become clear that the human lightbody is a necessary part of your human experience, even within the sacred space of the heart. It is what links the heart to the mind so that the heart can create within the mind.

There is a vast number of Mer-Ka-Ba geometrical patterns; over one hundred thousand are known throughout the universe. It has taken all life since the beginning of creation to understand and relate these forms of the Mer-Ka-Ba to existence and consciousness.

Humankind is working with only the first and second possible patterns, which are related to the star tetrahedron. Although there are many more, these other forms are not appropriate for human consciousness at this time, no matter what some people say. In fact, they would do harm instead of good.

In time, all will be revealed; nothing will be held back. Everything has its right time. You wouldn't let your three-year-old child drive a Mac truck, would you?

Combining the Sacred Space of the Heart with the Mer-Ka-Ba

I would like to share my experience around combining the sacred space of the heart with the Mer-Ka-Ba, because the story will explain a great deal. However, please know that when the time comes for you to have this experience, it will almost certainly be completely different from mine.

My experience almost seemed to be happening by accident, but of course, it was not an "accident." I sat breathing in the Mer-Ka-Ba meditation and had moved from there to my sacred space of the heart. I entered my cave and walked back to the space within the sacred space. I sat down inside the ring filled with bubbling, overflowing water and faced the wall—as I had done so many times before.

Not thinking of or feeling anything in particular, I began to simply be aware of my breathing, just feeling my breath. With my eyes open I looked at the stonewall in front of me. The wall became transparent, as

I had seen it do many times before—except this time, the space within the stones began to fill with a brilliant, white light. The light kept getting brighter until the cave disappeared and I was immersed in a solid white light field that I couldn't see out of. It was like being blinded.

This was very unusual and the first time I ever saw anything like this. I didn't experience fear. Nonetheless, my spine straightened and I was on full alert. I remember the energy rising in my body, which felt similar to the first time I experienced my Kundalini rising up my spine. There seemed to be no control. Whatever it was, it was just happening and it was very powerful.

Gradually, the white light receded, and I could see myself slowly emerging, or floating, out of the solid rock, through the surface of the planet, out into the space around it. It took me a minute to understand, but then it dawned on me that I was in my Mer-Ka-Ba field rising quickly into space.

Instinctively I knew that my sacred space of the heart and my Mer-Ka-Ba had somehow combined and merged into one, but I had no time to think about it.

I glanced back to see the area of this planet I had become so familiar with falling away behind me. I turned and looked out into the vast space of the stars and the seemingly equally vast space of the entire planet below me. I was both shocked and superexcited. What had caused this? I didn't know. What did this mean? I didn't know. I had no choice but to witness what was happening to me.

I was riding in a vehicle of ascension about a mile above the planet's surface, moving at a very rapid speed. Below me was a primitive world filled with jungle, forest, other vegetation and vast oceans, but still no animal life that I could see or sense. Just as I started thinking about getting closer to the surface, the vehicle of ascension descended, exactly as I had wanted.

Why was this happening? What was going on? So many questions were running through my head. Somehow I knew all of this was extremely important, yet as it was happening I could do nothing but experience and watch the scenes unfold.

And then I became aware of the presence of God all around me and within me and in the guiding principles that were giving me this experience, whatever they were. A knowingness came over me and answers to all my questions began to fill my understanding; an answer immediately followed each new question. I continued to soar above this planet feeling like I was being born into a brand-new universe I had never seen before. It was exhilarating!

Perhaps an hour went by and then I awoke as if from a dream, with the images and the feeling of where I'd been still lingering. For days, I could think of nothing else.

The Angels Explain

The angels came to me shortly after this experience. They appeared to be extremely delighted, and their light was brighter than I had ever seen it before. They told me that I had finally made it to the second level. Really, at that moment, I didn't understand what they were talking about, but I am a little slow sometimes.

My angels explained what had happened: The axis of my Mer-Ka-Ba and that of the toroidal field generated by my sacred space of the heart had aligned and become one. Another way to say it is that the toroidal fields of the Mer-Ka-Ba and the heart synchronized. Now, there are only about three inches between the axes of both fields, but those three inches might as well be three hundred miles, for they keep this experience from occurring at random; they keep the heart and the head apart until the time is right.

The angels also told me that this experience would be completely different for each person, but that it would help knowing about this possibility and to have patience. For some this synchronicity will happen quickly, whereas for others it may take years. However and whenever it happens, it will be perfect and for certain be in divine order.

Finally, they told me that when someone feels ready, it does help to try using both the imagination of the mind and the dreaming of the heart to see and feel the two axes coming together as one, but not to have any expectations. The timing is up to God, and there is nothing one can do to make this happen. It always depends on the "right" time.

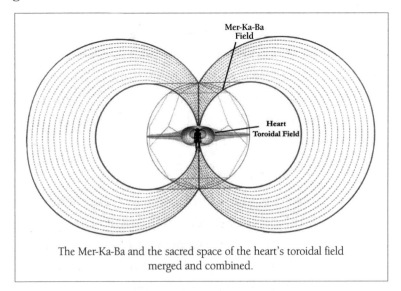

The Mer-Ka-Ba and the sacred space of the heart's toroidal field merged and combined.

Chapter Nine

Conscious Cocreation from the Heart Connected to the Mind

Thoth Speaks

Creating from the Heart

Creating from the Mind

Logic versus Feelings and Emotions

Dream a Dream of a New World

onscious cocreation starts with the knowledge of how to be within your Mer-Ka-Ba merged with your sacred space of the heart, with your spirit residing within the tiny space. From within this state of consciousness one directly creates and manifests out into the outer world. Know, however, that in this state creating is still limited, because the third level has not been attained. Still, it is the perfect place to begin learning.

What I would like to bring to your attention is the possibility of conscious cocreation within the small space of the sacred space of the heart. From this ancient place you can re-create the world into one of love and balance, healing all problems.

This possibility exists even if you are not aware of the Mer-Ka-Ba, but the Mer-Ka-Ba combined with the sacred space of the heart presents another plane of possibilities. Realize, though, that the full possibilities of human potential and conscious cocreation will not present themselves until all three levels are mastered—but we must start somewhere.

Thoth Speaks

Thoth and several other ascended masters, including his female counterpart, Shesat, had recently returned from the space/time/dimension beyond the "Great Wall," or the void between the octaves where humanity is now evolutionarily headed. Thoth's first name in ancient times was really a title, "Chiquetet", which means "seeker of wisdom." When Thoth returned from the next octave of universes, his personality had completely changed. His constant drive to understand reality had been replaced with a knowing that transcended his seeking, and he was so calm inside.

He appeared to me, looked at me and said: *"Drunvalo, we of the Earth have been seeking the relationship between human experience and creating since the beginning. We [meaning the ascended masters] have all tried to understand how human thought and actions and miracles were connected. For a while we thought we understood, but now we know there is more.*

"Now it is clear—when one creates from within the head using the mind, one is using a polarity instrument, the mind, to create with. And even though the intention is to create good in one way or another, the mind will always create both good and bad because that is its nature.

"I suggest that you try to create only from within the sacred space of the heart, for the heart knows only unity and will create the intention as it is conceived without its dark side."

This was a phenomenal revelation for me. I just stood there looking at Thoth and immediately knew the truth of what he was saying. I became excited—as I often do when I see something of importance—and could hardly wait to try out what he was suggesting.

Creating from the Heart

People have prayed to God to change the outer world's circumstances since the beginning of our awareness that God exists, but it seems as if God does not always listen to our prayers. Why? Have you ever asked yourself this question: Why does God not give us what we ask? In the Bible it says, "Ask, and you shall receive." But still it does not seem to happen. Perhaps what follows will provide an answer.

Let's talk about creation and creating. We are often taught both in school and at home that we are at the mercy of the elements and the random effects of the laws of physics. And of course, if you believe this to be true, then you are limited by this belief and it becomes your reality.

But long ago, people didn't think in this manner. They believed in a spiritual side to reality where the human spirit could change the outer reality by an inner intention.

In *The Isaiah Effect*, Gregg Braden reports on how in 1947 archaeologists found a document near the Dead Sea Scrolls called the Isaiah Scroll. The ancient Isaiah Scroll describes how humans have the power to influence future possibilities and prophecies and to change the world around us from within us.

Today, our techno-culture thinks this is fantasy. But is it? If we cannot influence the present and the future, then everything Jesus said to us has to be false. Didn't Jesus perform incredible feats such as changing the molecular construction of water into wine? He even brought a person back from the dead and made him alive again! Modern science believes that these kinds of stories are just that, stories, for there is little in science that supports such ideas.

Jesus said to us, "I say unto you, he that believeth in me, the works that I do shall he do also, and greater works than these shall he do." So what about the new children who are emerging all over the world? They are able to do the kinds of things Jesus could do, and science has documented this in such prestigious and popular periodicals as *Nature Journal* and *Omni Magazine*.

Scientists do not know how these children can create such amazing psychic phenomena, but they record that they are doing it. This is a fact. So how does the sacred space of the heart fit in with all this? Before I can explain, we must first look at how the mind creates a miracle and then compare this to how the sacred space of the heart does it.

Creating from the Mind

Often, when you pray to God for something you feel that is needed, nothing happens. The Isaiah Effect makes it clear why that is so. The ancient scrolls say that any miracle begins with attention, or focus of the mind—you place your mind's attention on what it is you want to see happen.

For example, let's say you want to heal yourself of a dreaded disease and therefore focus your thoughts on healing this particular part of your body. Of course, that is not enough for anything to actually happen, but it is an essential step to begin the healing process.

After the attention, you add intention. To continue our example, after you've placed your attention on the affected part of your body, you then have the intention of the disease going away.

But this is not enough, either. Three other parts must be involved or nothing happens—the mental body, the emotional body and the physical body.

The mental body, or mind, must see the body part being healed; it must hold the image of the body part being completely healed and healthy, with nothing wrong at all. And it must know for certain that this healing either is taking place now or that it will take place over a specific time frame, depending on what you can accept. Can you accept an instantaneous healing or does your belief pattern need more time? This knowing is essential, but still it is not enough.

Next the emotional body must engage. One must feel the emotion of what it will be like to be completely healthy, no longer having the disease. You must actually feel this emotion and not just have your mind thinking it is feeling the emotion. This is a tricky part for many, but without the emotional body engaged, absolutely nothing will happen.

And still it is not enough. You could be praying to be healed; your attention could be fully on the disease; your intention could be that the disease is healed; your mind could know that your body is either healed or going to be healed; and your emotional body could be feeling the emotion—say, joy—as if your body was completely healthy. But as long as the last and third part has not been engaged, nothing will happen.

How many people have prayed for something using all the above, just knowing it will happen, crying for hours for it to happen and still—nothing. This is because the last part has not been brought into the equation. It is the part that almost everyone forgets or doesn't recognize.

The final part, the forgotten aspect, is the physical body. In our example, you must feel the part of your body being completely normal

and healed. This does not mean feeling a mental pattern or consciousness searching within the body. Rather, this means having actual body
sensations where you feel your body responding. You feel no more
pain; instead you feel vitality in the area of your body you are focusing
on. You feel the health and beauty of your body. When this final step
of the body responding begins, the miracle will always follow.

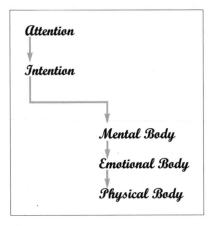

But there is more, which was not discussed in the *Isaiah Effect*, for
what Thoth is saying is that when we create from the mind, we create
both polarities of our intention. So if we pray for peace, for example,
we get both peace and war. This is exactly what we see in this world
today. Millions, if not billions of people are praying for and wanting
peace, but what we have are areas of the world in peace and areas of
the world in war, all mingled together. (At the moment, forty-six wars
are going on.) So let's look at this situation even deeper.

Logic versus Feelings and Emotions

The mind creates by using thoughts, and the thoughts follow one
another using logic. And so in whatever the mind creates, you can
logically follow the path of how the reality has been transformed from
one state to another. Even if it is a miracle, it still will have a logical
sequence if you can find it. But, as I have said, it will always gener-
ate both sides of the polarity of the original intention.

The heart, however, is completely different. The heart creates through dreams and images, and these manifest through feelings and emotions. This form of creation does not use logic and therefore does not have to be logical to get from one state to another.

If you are praying for rain using the heart, for example, it could start raining immediately even if there were no clouds in the sky only moments before. It is just like dreams, where you may find yourself in Italy in one scene and seconds later you are in Canada in a completely different scene. How did you get from Italy to Canada in a couple of seconds? Of course, we accept this happening in our dreams, but we think it is impossible in the 3D world. Perhaps it is not?!

Dream a Dream of a New World

One of the last pieces of information you need to consciously cocreate lies in the experiential realization that no matter how it appears to you, within the sacred space of the heart there will always be a direct connection back to the 3-D reality of the stars and planets. Sometimes this connection will not present itself immediately, but if you continue to enter your heart, you will find it.

This is very important, since it is this connection back to the stars and planets that allows the dreams of the heart to manifest in this world. So before you begin to manifest from within the sacred space of the heart, find the connection back to this world through the stars and planets so you know the truth.

So I ask you to go into your sacred space of the heart and merge your heart with your Mer-Ka-Ba field and begin dreaming a dream of a new, healthy world.

Apply all you know to consciously cocreate with God a new body, a new life and finally a new world. This power is your birthright and your heritage, for you are the son or daughter of God. From within your intimate relationship with God, all things are possible.

These instructions are a pathway to the realization that your body is light and the world you live within is light, and that both are directly connected to your consciousness. Living within your heart surrounded by the energy field of your Mer-Ka-Ba, living and creating from this holy place—this is the next step toward finally realizing the truth of who you really are and the beginning of the fulfillment of your sacred purpose for existing. At this point, you will certainly realize that you are in the process of ascension into heaven . . . And I want to close with the words of an old friend of us all:

"You may say I'm a dreamer, but I'm not the only one. Perhaps some day you'll join us, and the world will live as one." —*John Lennon*

When We Created the World

It was lonely being the only One
And so I made two.
And then there was you.
You were so beautiful with your eyes of innocence
but I loved you from afar and yet so very near
and I loved you in ways you could not comprehend.
You didn't know I was watching through the eyes of
every person you met,
Nor could you hear my voice in the wind.
You thought that the Earth was just dirt and rocks,
You didn't realize it was my body.
When you slept, we would meet in your heart
And make love with our spirits as One.
We would birth new worlds with such passion.
But when you were awake, you remembered nothing.
You thought it was just another dream.
It was just another day alone.
But in your heart I await you, my love, forever.
For the truth of our love and Oneness will always be.
Our love is the Matrix of All That Is.
Remember, Sweet One,
In your heart I will always await thee
In the place that is small.

—Drunvalo

For Further Reading

Braden, Greg. *The Isaiah Effect: Decoding the Lost Science of Prayer and Prophesy*. New York: Harmony Books, 2000.

Carlile, William H. "'Everything' Is on Table to Cut Valley Pollution." The Arizona Republic, 30 May 1996 (A1, A8).

Dong, Paul, and Thomas E. Rafill. *China's Super Psychics*. New York: Marlowe and Company, 1997.

Melchizedek, Drunvalo. *The Ancient Secret of the Flower of Life*. 2 vols. Flagstaff: Light Technology Publishing, 1998.

Twyman, James F. *Messages from Thomas: Raising a Psychic Child*. Forres: Findhorn Press, 2003.

For more information on the "Mindfold," go to www.spiritof maat.com.

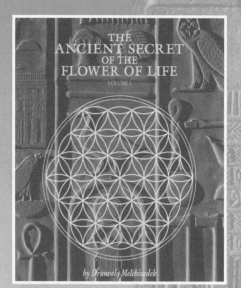

THE ANCIENT SECRET OF THE FLOWER OF LIFE
VOLUME 2

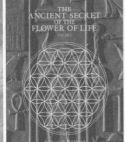

ISBN 1-891824-17-1
Soft cover, 228 p.

$25⁰⁰

⚙ **THE UNFOLDING OF THE THIRD INFORMATIONAL SYSTEM**
The Circles and Squares of Human Consciousness; Leonardo da Vinci's True Understanding of the Flower of Life; Exploring the Rooms of the Great Pyramid

⚙ **WHISPERS FROM OUR ANCIENT HERITAGE**
The Initiations of Egypt; the Mysteries of Resurrection; Interdimensional Conception; Ancient Mystery Schools; Egyptian Tantra, Sexual Energy and the Orgasm

⚙ **UNVEILING THE MER-KA-BA MEDITATION**
Chakras and the Human Energy System; Energy Fields around the Body; the Seventeen Breaths of the Mer-Ka-Ba Meditation; the Sacred Geometry of the Human Lightbody

⚙ **USING YOUR MER-KA-BA**
The Siddhis or Psychic Powers; Programming Your Mer-Ka-Ba; Healing from the Prana Sphere; Coincidence, Thought and Manifestation; Creating a Surrogate Mer-Ka-Ba

⚙ **CONNECTING TO THE LEVELS OF SELF**
Mother Earth and Your Inner Child; Life with Your Higher Self; How to Communicate with Everything; the Lessons of the Seven Angels

⚙ **TWO COSMIC EXPERIMENTS**
The Lucifer Experiment and the Creation of Duality; the 1972 Sirian Experiment and the Rebuilding of the Christ Consciousness Grid

⚙ **WHAT WE MAY EXPECT IN THE FORTHCOMING DIMENSIONAL SHIFT**
How to Prepare; Survival in the Fourth Dimension; the New Children

The sacred Flower of Life pattern, the primary geometric generator of all physical form, is explored in even more depth in this volume, the second half of the famed Flower of Life workshop. The proportions of the human body, the nuances of human consciousness, the sizes and distances of the stars, planets and moons, even the creations of humankind, are all shown to reflect their origins in this beautiful and divine image. Through an intricate and detailed geometrical mapping, Drunvalo Melchizedek shows how the seemingly simple design of the Flower of Life contains the genesis of our entire third-dimensional existence.

From the pyramids and mysteries of Egypt to the new race of Indigo children, Drunvalo presents the sacred geometries of the Reality and the subtle energies that shape our world. We are led through a divinely inspired labyrinth of science and stories, logic and coincidence, on a path of remembering where we come from and the wonder and magic of who we are.

Finally, for the first time in print, Drunvalo shares the instructions for the Mer-Ka-Ba meditation, step-by-step techniques for the re-creation of the energy field of the evolved human, which is the key to ascension and the next dimensional world. If done from love, this ancient process of breathing prana opens up for us a world of tantalizing possibility in this dimension, from protective powers to the healing of oneself, of others and even of the planet.

Available from your favorite bookstore or:

LIGHT TECHNOLOGY PUBLISHING
P.O. Box 3540
Flagstaff, AZ 86003
(928) 526-1345
(800) 450-0985
FAX (928) 714-1132
Or use our on-line bookstore:
www.lighttechnology.com

SPEAKS OF MANY TRUTHS AND ZOOSH THROUGH ROBERT SHAPIRO

SHAMANIC SECRETS for MATERIAL MASTERY
Learn to communicate with the planet

This book explores the heart and soul connection between humans and Mother Earth. Through that intimacy, miracles of healing and expanded awareness can flourish.

To heal the planet and be healed as well, we can lovingly extend our energy selves out to the mountains and rivers and intimately bond with the Earth. Gestures and vision can activate our hearts to return us to a healthy, caring relationship with the land we live on.

The character and essence of some of Earth's most powerful features is explored and understood, with exercises given to connect us with those places. As we project our love and healing energy there, we help the Earth to heal from man's destruction of the planet and its atmosphere. Dozens of photographs, maps and drawings assist the process in 25 chapters, which cover the Earth's more critical locations.

$19⁹⁵ SOFTCOVER 498P.
ISBN 1-891824-12-0

Chapter Titles:

SHAMANIC SECRETS for PHYSICAL MASTERY

COMING SOON

The purpose of this book is to allow you to understand the sacred nature of your own physical body and some of the magnificent gifts it offers you. When you work with your physical body in these new ways, you will discover not only its sacredness, but how it is compatible with Mother Earth, the animals, the plants, even the nearby planets, all of which you now recognize as being sacred in nature. It is important to feel the value of oneself physically before one can have any lasting physical impact on the world. The less you think of yourself physically, the less likely your physical impact on the world will be sustained by Mother Earth.

If a physical energy does not feel good about itself, it will usually be resolved; other physical or spiritual energies will dissolve it because it is unnatural. The better you feel about your physical self when you do the work in the previous book as well as this one and the one to follow, the greater and more lasting will be the benevolent effect on your life, on the lives of those around you and ultimately on your planet and universe. SOFTCOVER 600P.

$19⁹⁵   ISBN 1-891824-29-5

Chapter Titles:

- Cellular Clearing of Traumas, Unresolved Events
- Cellular Memory
- Identifying Your Body's Fear Message
- The Heart Heat Exercise
- Learn Hand Gestures
  —Remove Self-Doubt
  —Release Pain or Hate
  —Clear the Adrenals or Kidneys
  —Resolve Sexual Dysfunction
- Learning the Card Technique for Clarifying Body Message
- Seeing Life as a Gift
- Relationship of the Soul to Personality
- The New Generation of Children
- The Creator and Religions
- Food, Love & Addictions

- Communication of the Heart
- Dreams & Their Significance
- The Living Prayer/Good Life
- Life Force and Life Purpose
- Physical Mastery
- His Life/
  Mandate
  for His
  Ancestors/
  Importance of
  Animals/ Emissaries
- Physical Mastery
- Talking to Rain/
  Bear Claw Story
- Disentanglement
- Grief Culture
- Closing Comments

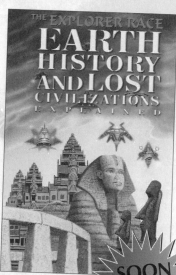

Peace to All Beings

$14.95
$16.50 CANADA

SEDONA
Journal of EMERGENCE!

2004
AND YOU

Predictions Book

Announcing a special book

2004 PREDICTIONS

available for Oct. 2003

Note: Author photos as appeared on 2003 edition.

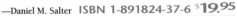

Ultimate UFO Books:
ANDROMEDA

By the Andromedans and Zoosh through Robert Shapiro

Including the complete, orignal text of the **Wendelle Stevens** *book Andromeda*

A group of Andromedans visited a University of Mexico professor of physics and atomic energy, Professor Hernandez (not his real name), in the 1970s and early 1980s. He was given **HIGHLY TECHNICAL** information on a method to manufacture a shield around any jet plane, which would allow the pilot and passengers to **FLY TO MARS** or whatever planet or star they wanted to reach, in comfort and safety. But because of the professor's life situation, the country he was in, the times and other factors, he was not able to use the information, which would have made him wealthy and would have allowed **EARTH ASTRONAUTS** to explore the planets and stars safely. After many visits from the ETs and an expansion in consciousness, he was committed to a mental institution. Shortly after he was released, he was last seen sitting in a park near his home in his walking shorts reading a newspaper. He never returned to his home that day—he disappeared forever. His journals were taken and the information from the Andromedans was never made public.

Now, speaking through **SUPERCHANNEL ROBERT SHAPIRO**, the Andromedans who contacted the professor tell us what really happened, and give the instructions about the shielding technology so that scientists who have the background can use it, and they also clear up all the questions one would have after reading the Spanish or English book. They also supply a lively account of their lives and **OTHER ADVENTURES** they had when they came to Earth. Each crew member of the spaceship speaks: Leia the social diplomat, the scientific liason, the two scientists—and then as an extra treat, Leia's daughter and her playmate contribute to the story.

$16.^{95}$ Softcover   ISBN 1-891824-35-X

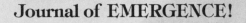